FAITH UNDERSTOOD

*An Ordinary Man's Journey
to the Presence of God*

Paul Zucarelli

Faith Understood: An Ordinary Man's Journey to the Presence of God

Published by Zucarelli Family Faith Charitable Trust
Fountain Hills, Arizona 85268 USA

ISBN: 978-0-692-15316-1 (paperback)
ISBN: 978-0-692-16375-7 (ebook)
LCCN: 2018908737

Cover photo: Michael Zucarelli

rev201902

DEDICATION

This book is dedicated to my entire family, along with all its future generations. May you come to know God, Jesus Christ, and the Holy Spirit. Remember to carry your cross daily, because at the end of your mortal life it will only be between you and God. All that matters is to live a life focused on the salvation of your soul through Jesus Christ. Human death is the beginning of eternal life which I have been called to witness.

The book is also dedicated to anyone who has a burning desire to know whether God, His unconditional love for you, and the heavenly realm exists. I testify to this. I hope this book fills your need to know.

Finally and most importantly, this book is dedicated to the glory of God, whose merciful grace has granted me a second chance while on this earth to do His will.

Jesus said to her, "I am the resurrection and the life; he who believes in me, though he die, yet shall he live, and whoever lives and believes in me shall never die. Do you believe this?" (John 11:25–26)

TABLE OF CONTENTS

FOREWORD

For I know the plans I have for you, declares the LORD, plans for welfare and not for evil, to give you a future and a hope.

JEREMIAH 29:11

Paul Zucarelli's story shows us that God has a plan for our lives filled with hope. This plan always involves the convergence of many different people and events. Little did I know on Pentecost morning 2017 that God's plan for Paul's life would deeply connect him to mine and the Diocese of Phoenix. God's plan led Paul's son Michael to seek prayers for his father at St. Paul's Church, where I happened to be celebrating Mass. God's plan and Michael's plea moved me to continue to pray for Paul the rest of the day. God's plan brought Paul from near certain death to a restored life. Most importantly God is now using this story to build up His kingdom through Paul's witness to the living Jesus Christ. I hope you are encouraged by Paul's story as much as I have been.

This book is not so much an autobiography as it is a witness that God is working in our lives. Paul's story is one of trust in God during the most difficult of times. Paul is a successful businessman who worked his way from extensive college debt to great success in the business world. Throughout his business career, a more important journey was taking place—a journey of faith. Paul went from doing good deeds for God to realizing that faith is a relationship with God, whose love at work in us can accomplish far more than we could hope for or imagine. Paul's journey is one of the heart. He has learned many lessons along the way, lessons that will help everyone who reads this book come to deeper faith in the Lord.

I hope that Paul's story encourages you to experience the reality of God's love and to welcome Him as the Lord of your life. God has a plan for your life, and as St. Paul says, "We know that for those who love God all things work together for good, for those who are called according to his purpose" (Romans 8:28). Paul witnesses that God takes even our greatest trials and our greatest difficulties and uses them to draw us closer to Him.

I rejoice that Paul's close brush with death has become a fruitful means of evangelization in the Diocese of Phoenix. Paul's story has touched my heart, and I hope it touches yours as well.

+Thomas J. Olmsted
Bishop of Phoenix

INTRODUCTION

Like you, I am an ordinary person. I simply have had an extraordinary experience. Many highly educated folks label what happened to me as a "near-death experience." Personally, I see it as a joyful blessing to be shared. I have been given a second opportunity to live, and I am abundantly grateful for the gift of life, yet I now look at life from a very different perspective.

It is difficult to write a book about yourself. In fact, it is both humbling and painful when you are reduced to writing facts and observations of your life. Nonetheless, many dear friends and the clinical personnel at the Mayo Clinic have urged me to do so. Along the way I've struggled to write words that would somehow communicate the meaning behind the thoughts, emotions, and factual events that actually occurred.

One night in October 2017, I opened the Bible to a random page. My eyes focused on the far right of the page to 1 Corinthians 2:1–5 and I read the Apostle Paul's words:

> *When I came to you, brethren, I did not come
> proclaiming to you the testimony of God in lofty
> words or wisdom. For I decided to know nothing*

among you except Jesus Christ and him crucified.
And I was with you in weakness and in much fear
and trembling; and my speech and my message
were not in plausible words of wisdom, but in
demonstration of the Spirit and of power, that your
faith might not rest in the wisdom of men but in the
power of God.

This Scripture motivated me to create this book. It is really not a story about me. Rather, it is a story about faith, God, and spirituality. All of us will face trials, pain, suffering, and inevitably physical death. Although many have written about near-death experiences, my story focuses on how the convergence of faith, prayer, hope, and God's grace intervened in my life. The "connect the dots" in my story are beyond human comprehension. What I experienced was the power of God and the demonstration of the Spirit as St. Paul referenced. After I read this scripture reference, I picked up a pen and began to write this book, encouraged by the Holy Spirit.

For Christians, I pray that this book will strengthen, confirm, and validate your faith and hope in the Lord. For readers who do not believe or are uncertain, I pray that your heart and mind will be opened to receiving a message of God's love, Jesus Christ's mercy, and the sheer power of the Holy Spirit. The simple truth is that God exists and we have a soul. We each must make a personal decision to accept God's existence and whether we will have continued life in the spirit beyond the human body.

INTRODUCTION

May this book demonstrate—through my testimony—how real and powerful faith truly is. I praise and thank God for allowing me a second chance to continue life in my earthly body. I pray that my story may embolden your faith and deepen your relationship with God and humanity. Please keep your heart open to what God is calling you to do as you read my testimony. And remember, I am just an ordinary person like you.

May God almighty be given all praise and glory.

CHAPTER ONE

THE EARLY YEARS—FAITH'S PREPARATION

For I am not ashamed of the gospel. It is the power of God for salvation to everyone who believes...For in it the righteousness of God is revealed from faith to faith; as it is written, the one who is righteous by faith will live.
ROMANS 1:16–17

I was born on April 15, 1959, in Buffalo, New York. My dad, Robert Anthony Zucarelli, was Catholic, and my mom, Avis Muriel Zeims, was Protestant. Our family attended St. Margaret's Parish in Buffalo, New York. Like most children, I went to public school from K–12. When I was eleven years old, my math teacher, Mrs. Prior, asked me to stay after class. I vividly remember her saying, "Paul, I see something special in you. Have you accepted Jesus Christ as your Savior and Lord?" (Try doing that in today's public schools!)

I really held this teacher in high esteem, so I asked her what I was supposed to do in order to accomplish this. She told me that before I went to bed that evening, I should simply invite Jesus into my life as Lord and accept him as my Savior. And kneeling at my bedside that night, I did exactly as she instructed. This was a foundational moment in my life, a simple act by a teacher who affirmed me as a person began my redemptive journey. At such a young age, I didn't comprehend nor understand how critically important this simple act of faith would become in my life.

Shortly after this, our family moved to the suburbs of Buffalo, where I completed eighth grade and entered high school. During high school, my mother, who was in her early forties, was diagnosed with breast cancer. She received a radical mastectomy as treatment. However, a year later the medical community informed her that the cancer had appeared in the other breast. The physicians suggested that she get her affairs in order. My mom decided to have no further medical treatment; instead she turned to prayer, diligently asking God to allow her to live and see her children grow up as well as her potential grandchildren. One evening she went to the Nativity of the Blessed Virgin Mary Church for healing of her cancer. There at a charismatic Catholic prayer meeting, Holy Spirit-filled believers laid hands on her and prayed for her healing. She shared that she felt what was like a bolt of lightning go through her chest. God miraculously healed her!

She convinced my dad to move to Tucson, Arizona, as she had a cousin there and she liked the desert. She lived another forty years cancer-free. She *never* saw another doctor until she was in her seventies and needed cataract surgery, a knee replacement, and a few other unrelated medical procedures. She died peacefully on June 21, 2015, at the age of eighty-three, having seen her grown grandchildren and one great grandchild.

God answers prayers.

Although my parents moved to Tucson in 1978, my two siblings and I were at different stages of life. My older brother, Steven, enlisted in the Air Force and left home. My younger sister, Donna, was still in high school and moved with our parents to Tucson. As the middle child, I was just finishing high school and had been accepted at Canisius College, a Jesuit college in Buffalo. I had also been dating my childhood sweetheart, Mary Beth Dailey, since the age of fifteen. Thus, I decided to remain in Buffalo and go to the Jesuit College.

My family couldn't afford room and board on campus, so I spent several years living with Carl and Pat Moll, who were very dear friends of my parents. I worked as a waiter to pay my living expenses. The Molls had three living children, and their oldest son, Thomas, was my age. Since there was very little room to add me to their family, I slept on a cot in Tom's room. He was a saint to put up with me. The entire Moll family was wonderfully compassionate to me during my time at Canisius College. I contributed what I could to their household expenses. Their graciousness to me was a gift.

While attending college, I was fascinated by the dialogue I had with the Jesuit priests on faculty at Canisius. The priest that most fascinated me was Fr. Johan Ladislaus Uhas. A European priest, he was a tremendous philosopher of life and teacher of the gospel. I began to learn at a very deep level what Christianity really meant and its impact on one's heart, mind, and soul while studying theology classes. Learning about the historical

Jesus Christ as Divine and human left a profound impact on such a young man as myself. By learning about the Trinity at Canisius, I began to take a keen interest in becoming a priest myself. This was short-lived, however, because of my deep desire to marry Beth (as Mary Beth was known) and start a family. Nonetheless, I learned more about Christianity and stewardship in my four years at Canisius than I did by going to Mass my entire life. It was all part of my growth and my journey. I believe God places people in our lives to learn from if we are open to growing as individuals and particularly in our faith. In other words, we are built for productive relationships with one another; we are meant to live in community with one another.

I remained in Buffalo until graduating in 1981 with my degree in accounting. Upon graduation, I had amassed $32,000 in student loans and had no savings for repaying them. What I did have was a belief in myself that I could make my way and earn a living. I had lived by observing what both good and bad character looked like in other people's behaviors and actions. I tried to emulate the good observations and pattern my life accordingly. Simultaneously, I applied antithetical learning to the bad observations—namely, how not to behave.

Having significant debt at a young age taught me that I had earned my education through discipline, hard work, and a lot of perseverance. I knew I did not reach this milestone of a college degree alone. Looking back on my life, the encouragement of my parents, the support of many teachers, and the innate desire to grow through learning all worked together for the Lord's greater purpose. I leaned on my faith as I moved out into the world after graduation. This type of blind faith is simply trust. God has a plan for the good works he wants us to do in our lives. He knew us before we were formed in our mother's womb. He has also destined each of us for his greater purpose. As the Apostle Paul states:

For we are His (God's) workmanship, created in Christ Jesus for the good works which God has prepared beforehand, that we should walk in them. (Ephesians 2:10)

Little did I know at the time, the $32,000 student loan debt was a blessing! I knew I had to pay this back as it represented other people's investments in me as a person. It was the beginning of another important life lesson—namely, stewardship.

By May 1981, I had an accounting degree and wanted to sit immediately for the CPA exam since I had accepted a job in Tucson with Coopers & Lybrand as a staff accountant. I vividly recall asking my father to lend me five hundred dollars so I could quit my job as a waiter. The money would cover my living expenses for the month while I studied for the CPA exam. My father, with a lot of love and pride, did so without hesitation. I got through the exam and passed it. I now was ready and prepared to enter my professional life. This is where preparation and preparedness meets opportunity. (More on this in a bit.)

Beth and I got married on July 11, 1981, at The

Nativity of the Blessed Virgin Mary Church in Harris Hill, New York, the same church where my mother received her charismatic healing. It was the culmination of a relationship that began in 1975. After our wedding, Beth and I moved to Tucson, as it held better job opportunities than Buffalo since the country was still in an economic recession at that time. Also, my parents had relocated to Tucson, so we had some family nearby to help us if needed. My mom's faith continued to expand and grow due to her cancer diagnosis and her prayers to live a full life. She was a testament of complete faith in Christ. Never wavering, always working hard, she continued to live with conviction that the Lord would provide health to her body.

So, with a new marriage and a new job 2,300 miles away, Beth and I drove to Tucson to start our life together. I prayed that it would all work out. When you are an adolescent or a young adult, you are caught up in the youthful activities of life. God, Jesus, and faith had to fit in somewhere, but quite honestly these were minimized given my available time. I was focused on providing for my new wife and simply working hard. When I started my new job at Coopers & Lybrand, I was thrown into a "learn it and perform or leave" environment. No training—just go figure it out.

My primary industry clients were healthcare and mining. I was fascinated by healthcare—namely, hospitals, doctors, and nurses working in the ministry of healing. However, I only worked in public accounting for a few years. A new industry was forming called managed healthcare. Its cornerstone was health maintenance and prevention. I ended up going to work as the assistant controller for the State of Arizona's first Health Maintenance Organization, Pima Care, in 1983.

Pima Care was a group model HMO that promised lower premiums, expanded benefits (including wellness), and preventative services at virtually no cost to the consumer. Its limitation was that the care was highly coordinated and managed via a narrow network of highly engaged healthcare providers. I later became the chief financial officer of the company. I was able to provide for my wife, and she and I bought our first home and prepared to have children. What started as blind faith in 1981 upon graduation from college was now transitioning into how to be a loving husband while providing for my soon-to-be expanding family. I cherished this responsibility, and I knew that somehow, if I worked hard and prayed, God would take care of our family.

CHAPTER TWO

THE BUSYNESS OF LIFE—A FAMILY MAN

Commit your work to the Lord, and your plans will be established.
A man's mind plans his way, but the Lord directs his steps.
PROVERBS 16:3, 9

We were blessed with our first son on May 8, 1983. We easily agreed that his name would be Michael. I can honestly attest that there is nothing greater in this world than witnessing the birth of your child—a human being created by a loving God for us to raise and teach. It was a joyous time wrought with tremendous responsibilities, and it changed me as a person for the better. No longer did I think about just me and my wife, but rather future generations too.

Meanwhile, the company I worked for was sold, and my work position was tenuous with the new, out-of-state owner. At a ripe age of twenty-five, life kept coming at me in waves of constant change. My early years in the business world taught me that shrewdness, cunning, and self-interest were often rewarded. Frankly, selfishness prevailed. Granted, I occasionally witnessed compassion, kindness, and humility, values I esteemed. Unfortunately, however, these were few and far between. Despite the ac-quiring company offering me an opportunity to relocate,

I did not have matching values with the new owners. I began to interview elsewhere.

Better is the poor man who walks in his integrity than a rich man who is perverse in his ways (Proverbs 28:6)

On December 16, 1986, Beth and I were blessed with the birth of our second son, David. Once again, we experienced the joyful feeling of a newborn child. My wife and I agreed on his name quickly as well; we knew we wanted both our sons to have strong biblical names. We wanted to give them something to reflect on and rely on as they grew older. Michael in Hebrew means, "Who is like God?" and also was the name of an archangel identified in the Bible, and David (also Hebrew) means "beloved." Through the lineage of King David, we received the Son of Man, Jesus Christ—God himself.

Upon the conception and birth of both our sons, I prayed when I could for divine guidance in order to be a good father and provider. In my twenties, these prayers were ill-defined. I simply asked the Lord for healthy children. I promised God that I would dedicate time to help less fortunate children in society as a demonstration of my gratitude for our sons, who were both healthy upon birth. I also joined the Arizona Children's Association's board of directors, which served to help children who were abused, neglected, abandoned, or simply needing assistance due to inadequate family resources or infrastructure.

I worried about my ability to be an adequate father, provider, and husband, given my young age. I had started a new job, I had two sons, my wife was a homemaker, and I felt tremendous pressure. I had a lot of responsibilities as an executive, and I felt overwhelmed. I was really scared. I needed clarity and direction about my purpose.

One weekend, I drove alone to the highest mountain peak near Tucson—Mt. Lemmon, elevation 9,159 feet—where I sat under a tall pine tree and contemplated life. Alone, contemplative time is powerful. In stillness and quiet I reflected on what was really important in my life. I also examined my own conscience. That day I sought guidance, special providence, and direction from above to guide my life. In essence, I needed a "path," and I prayed for this divine direction. After half a day spent in soul searching and prayer, I wrote my personal mission statement that day at the top of a mountain. It is clear to me only now that what I wrote was influenced by the Holy Spirit. I wanted to put in writing "who" I was and "what" I stood for as a person and "how" I was to live my life. Although I didn't fully realize it at the time, my mission statement dealt with my stewardship roles and how to serve God and others. It was—and still is to this day—all about relationships, roles, responsibilities, and serving. Little did I know at the time how this simple exercise would be relevant three decades later. You can find my mission statement at the back of this book.

I have been a very blessed man. God places people and events before us to grow as Christians and increase our hope, and increased hope strengthens faith. There is deep meaning in reflection of our past if we are honest with ourselves. The true meaning of life becomes real when we become contemplative.

There are two events that continue to mark my soul concerning our sons. When Michael was born, we had moved to a new home with an in-ground pool. I built a fenced-in wooden play yard adjacent to the pool for him. It was about 20 feet by 12 feet. A gate connected his play yard with the pool area. The gate had a latch at 5 feet in height. Michael was about three years old and highly intelligent. One Saturday my father unexpectedly came over to visit. Michael was in his play yard and Dad and I were visiting in the great room which faced the pool area with a sliding glass door to the backyard. Meanwhile, Beth was on the phone in the kitchen. As my dad and I conversed, he interrupted me to ask about Michael's whereabouts. I said he was in his play yard. My father replied, "I just saw a tennis ball go into the pool, and I thought I saw Michael near the pool."

I jumped up, ran outside, and there, in the deep end of the pool, was Michael underwater and struggling. We pulled him from the water, thankful that he was fine even though he had been submerged for about thirty seconds. Our intelligent son Michael had pushed a tall toy over to the gate, stood on it, and opened the latch to the gate and threw the tennis ball towards the pool. Then he tried to reach into the pool to retrieve the ball and fell in. If my dad hadn't come over unexpectedly that Saturday morning, at that time, we may have lost our oldest son to a drowning.

Every event is part of the Master's plan. We had God's intervention that day—or a guardian angel at the least!

The second indelible mark on my soul concerned our other son, David. When David was about six years old, I decided to take him up to Mt. Lemmon, Arizona, to play in the snow. (Snow is a big deal for kids who live in the desert!) I had bought him a saucer that a child sits on, holds on to two straps and slides downhill over the snow. He was so excited to try out his new saucer. We drove to an area near the top of the mountain, and there was a large clearing with few pine trees in the distance. I assumed it would be a good place to have David saucer down. Not having ever done this before, I didn't realize how fast the saucer would go with a child on it. In retrospect, the hill I chose was way too steep; I just didn't know it. I sat David on the saucer, let go, and he began his one (and only!) downhill decent. Within seconds I realized that the combination of his weight and the hill slope was extremely dangerous; gravity propelled him at a very high rate of speed.

As David began to scream, I panicked. I yelled to him to jump off the saucer. He continued downhill, picking up speed. He had traveled about two hundred yards in a clear area of snow when I suddenly noticed two large Ponderosa pine trees directly in his path. The trees were each about two feet wide, ten feet apart and fifty feet tall, and David was heading straight for them. The saucer hit the left tree head on, and I saw David's body literally eject toward the right side of the tree, and he went flying in the air between the two trees. He landed and began to tumble until his body lay still in a snow pile.

My heart sank in my chest as I saw my boy's body lying motionless. I ran to him, and he moaned. I asked him to lay still and move his arms and legs only. He complied. Amazingly, he sat up and said his back hurt a little, but he was not seriously injured. I thanked God he was not hurt, and we drove home. I blamed myself for this episode—I should have known better. Why his body went to the right to avoid the tree while the saucer impacted dead center on the tree is a mystery, but yet another blessing from God. The Holy Spirit dwells within each of us to guide us. God's protection is real for those who choose to acknowledge Him. Both boys escaped tragedy at a young age through divine intervention. Looking back on one's life provides deep clarity of how God protects each of us.

May the God of peace himself sanctify you wholly; and may your spirit and soul and body be kept sound and blameless at the coming of our Lord Jesus Christ. He who calls you is faithful, and he will do it. (1 Thessalonians 5:23–24)

Beth has done a tremendous job raising our sons. She routinely went back to work at times when I changed careers and positions. Never complaining, she did what the family needed whenever the family needed it. Undoubtedly, she has had the more important role in the family as she instilled values, morals, and ethics into our children. As they developed biologically, so did their souls under her direction.

As for me, I felt a constant need to grow, learn, and innovate as a person. I changed careers four times, and each time God blessed me with professional and personal growth and success. I have always strived to help and serve others. This is at my core as a human being. Perhaps that is why I chose service industries as my career. Creating opportunities for others, adding jobs, and allowing people to not only understand their human potential but fulfill it brought me great joy. Nothing gave me more satisfaction than helping others succeed, both as individuals and within the work setting. God has truly blessed me during my work career. God, family, and work—in that order—have always been my priorities. In my pursuit of God, Jesus Christ is the only way.

Although I started my career as a CPA, it became clearly evident that my vocation was healthcare. I recall in elementary school in Buffalo, I was interviewed by a reporter and had my picture and quotes published in the *Buffalo Evening News*. The question was one posed to all children: "What do you want to do when you grow up?" My answer was "To be a doctor so I can help people."

My family did not have the means to send me to medical school, nor did I know how to pursue this on my own, so I became an accounting major. But the passion for healthcare burned within me. After leaving Coopers & Lybrand to work for the only HMO operating in Arizona, I was approached by a nonprofit health organization to start a new health plan from the ground up and was recruited to be the executive director. I was twenty-seven years old. As executive director, I was the first employee hired. There were no co-workers, no customers, and no revenue. The board gave me a blank piece of paper and said, "Go." Why they picked me, only God knows.

Talk about a leap of faith! The challenge was that the company had no customers or revenue. My dad encouraged me to "take the risk" and step out into the unknown. I prayed about it and accepted the job. I was promoted to president of the company within a few years, and it became one of the largest provider-sponsored health insurance companies in the United States. We helped many people over my eleven-year tenure.

When healthcare reform failed at a national level politically in the mid 1990s, the nonprofit hospitals and physicians sold the company to United Healthcare. The provider-owners knew they could demand higher fees for their services if they didn't own a health plan that was accountable to its community for costs. Selling the health plan to a publically traded insurance company also added another layer of profits to shareholders and future premiums.

The provider-owners negotiated long-term contracts to provide care well above general inflationary levels once United Healthcare owned the health plan. I resigned as soon as the sale transaction closed. I knew with provider fees guaranteed to increase over the years, along with United Healthcare's needs for shareholder return, premiums would double within five to ten years. Once again, the Lord directed me to where I needed to be.

I took my severance pay and started looking for new

opportunities. I then entered the employee benefit business, where I helped employers and individuals purchase health insurance or self-insure their workforce. I became the president of CBIZ Benefits and Insurance Services, Arizona. I was back in the healthcare industry, serving people's needs and blessed to work for a fine company.

My thirties and forties went quickly. Children, activities, schooling, friendships, neighbors, and so on filled my life. Staying true to my mission statement, I paid off our home mortgage at age thirty-seven and was debt-free. Funny how when you write something down, it gets done!

When I was in my early fifties, I reviewed my mission statement. As I read what I'd written twenty-five years ago, I felt I had accomplished my entire mission. When I mentioned this to a dear priest friend and spiritual mentor, Fr. Patrick Kennedy, he reminded me that our mission is never done. He asked me to reread my mission statement, and he pointed out that my mission statement was really all relationship-based. It all centered around relationships with other human beings. How could I possibly achieve my mission when people's lives are constantly growing, changing and in need? I felt re-energized after speaking to Fr. Kennedy. He reminded me to walk as a disciple of Christ and told me that many more people would be brought across my path for me to help.

A few years later, I had the privilege of taking care of my mother who was suffering from Alzheimer's. As we provided for her medical and safety needs, we witnessed firsthand how debilitating a disease this really is. We eventually hired round-the-clock caregivers to be with her in an assisted living facility so her safety and security were ensured. On Father's day, June 21, 2015, Beth and I were at church and the choir was singing "Ave Maria," one of Mom's favorites. I suddenly had this "sense" that Mom was passing away, which I shared with Beth. We went to visit her after church, and she passed away later that afternoon, finally at peace with the Lord. As she was approaching physical death and still conscious, all she wanted to do was hold my hand. Reflecting on this, the only real "need" at the end is for human contact or touch and knowing a loved one is near. Witnessing my mother's death taught me there is human dignity in passing from this earthly life to eternity.

CHAPTER THREE

LESSONS ALONG THE WAY—MIRACLES AND BLESSINGS OVERLOOKED

"For to this you have been called, because Christ suffered for you, leaving an example, that you should follow in his steps."
I PETER 2:21

After my mom passed, I began my own personal journey of health trials. I began to have symptoms of Atrial Fibrillation (AFib). This is an arrhythmia issue of one's heart which could have many causes. For me, it stemmed from having a heart murmur or mitral valve prolapse.

I had been initially diagnosed with a heart murmur upon a routine physical when I was twenty-four or twenty-five years old by a wonderful man, Dr. Vince McKenzie. He called it mitral valve regurgitation and said it was not uncommon. I lived an active lifestyle, playing various sports while growing up and routinely exercising. I had never had any problems other than getting winded easily under heavy exertion. Couple this with a Type A personality and . . . well, you get the picture.

However, when I was forty-eight years old, during the summer of 2007, one day I played golf in Madison, Wisconsin, in 90 degree heat with 95 percent humidity.

It was a hilly course, and I was hot and sweaty. At the end of nine holes, I drank an ice-cold 32-oz Gatorade. Within minutes, my heart rate felt totally out of sync. I finished the round, flew home the next morning, and returned to work—the whole time not feeling well. Something wasn't right. Yet because I was in such good physical shape, I functionally soldiered on. I waited a week before finally going to my internist, Dr. Gary Bohay. He checked my blood pressure and pulse and asked me if I felt lightheaded. I said I just didn't feel well, so he did an EKG. That showed I was in AFib, and he sent me immediately to a cardiologist two miles away. The cardiologist did another EKG, which confirmed AFib. He told me he wanted to do an ablation procedure, but after hearing what the procedure involved, I graciously declined.

My symptoms of atrial fibrillation abated on their own that week. I agreed to have some diagnostic and noninvasive tests with the cardiologist—consisting of an echo and stress test. He again confirmed mitral valve regurgitation. So, I assumed my AFib was an isolated event.

So, like many patients who encounter the medical community, I had various doctors bantering around terms like AFib and mitral valve regurgitation very nonchalantly. I needed time to digest what they were talking about; I knew God only gave me one heart. Atrial fibrillation is an abnormal heart rhythm characterized by rapid and irregular beating of the atria chamber of the heart. Mitral valve regurgitation is a disorder of the heart in which the mitral valve inside the heart does not close properly when the heart pumps out blood. It is the abnormal leaking of blood backwards from the left ventricle, through the mitral valve into the left atrium. Once I understood the diagnosis, I also learned that there are specialists who only see patients who suffer from AFib.

I then went to the University of Arizona Medical Center to see an electrophysiology cardiologist specializing in AFib. I was her patient from about 2008 to 2014. During my time with her as a patient, I went into AFib about once a year. When in AFib, I tried a medication called Flecainide, which sometimes worked to normalize my heart rhythm. Several other times they performed cardioversion, an electrical shock administered in an outpatient hospital setting. This routinely was successful in restoring normal heart rhythm.

The physician at the University of Arizona was very good; however, the bulk of her time was devoted to clinic research and not full-time patient care. In late 2014 I began going to a local cardiologist with a large cardiac group. My bouts of AFib were becoming more frequent, going from once a year to two to three times a year. To prevent or reduce the risk of stroke, the new doctor prescribed the drug Xeralto (a blood thinner) immediately upon AFib onset along with Flecainide twice a day until I converted on my own. The medication normally did the trick after four days on the drug regimen.

During 2016 I really did not feel well. I couldn't specifically say why; I thought I was just plain getting old and slowing down. My blood pressure would spike unexpectedly for a period of several hours. I had no energy, experienced shortness of breath, and my AFib was occurring more regularly. Close friends told me I looked pale. At an office visit on December 8, 2016, the cardiologist suggested I take Flecainide permanently to potentially avoid going into AFib. He also said he wanted to increase the dosage of my blood pressure medication. I had never had hypertension or high blood pressure, so I wondered what was really going on with me. I noticed a change in my demeanor; I was growing increasingly pensive and had a lack of well-being. Suddenly I thought, *Wait a minute—why am I treating symptoms through medication? And why does my health appear to be rapidly deteriorating?* I asked God for guidance. On my way home from that appointment, I heard an inner voice instructing me to call the Mayo Clinic for a second opinion as soon as I got home. The voice was that specific —the Mayo Clinic!

> *"So shall my word be that goes forth from my mouth; it shall not return to me empty, but it shall accomplish that which I purpose, and prosper in the thing for which I sent it." (Isaiah 55:11)*

There was a Mayo clinic located in Phoenix, 120 miles from where we lived. As soon as I got home I called Mayo and made an appointment for December 23, 2016, with a cardiologist named Dr. Simper. Mayo promptly took care of getting all my medical records, and when I arrived for my second opinion appointment, Dr. Simper had a towering stack of medical records beside him. He spent over an hour with me and confirmed that the AFib episodes were most likely caused by mitral valve regurgitation. He also stated that in his professional opinion, I most likely would need mitral valve surgery in the future. He wanted to perform a new cardiac stress test and echocardiogram, and thcsc were done on December 28, 2016. I passed the stress test, but the echo results showed I had a moderate-plus level of mitral valve leakage. Dr. Simper told me I most likely would need valve surgery due to my shortness of breath, fatigue, and general feeling of malaise. I felt God had sent me to Mayo, and I began to understand that surgery would be part of His plan.

I went into AFib again on April 10, 2017, and took Flecainide for two days and converted via the drug. Dr. Simper recommended that, due to the more active AFib episodes, I should stay on 150 mg of Flecainide for one week and then taper off to 75 mg. I had another bout of AFib on April 19, and again on April 28. This was very concerning, as I could not function while in AFib. I was taking my blood thinner Xarelto as well. With Flecainide in my system, I took another 75 mg immediately and converted each time in eight hours. Dr. Simper immediately referred me to Dr. Mulpuru, his electrophysiology cardiologist colleague at Mayo. When I saw Dr. Mulpuru on May 3, he recommended managing the AFib with different medications. He said he believed I was not quite ready for mitral valve surgery and that we should try and manage the AFib through medication for a year or two instead. I expressed my deep concern that I hadn't felt well for over a year and had no physical energy. I mentioned that my own research indicated the average

age for mitral valve surgery for a male is sixty-three, and I was fifty-eight. I felt led to advocate for myself—I knew in my soul that I needed to speak up at that moment.

"For the Holy Spirit will teach you in that very hour what you ought to say." (Luke 12:12)

I told Dr. Mulpuru, "Heart valves wear out. Surgeons either repair them if possible or replace them if they are not repairable, and repairs have better outcomes than replacements. Correct?"

He agreed, and I added, "If my valve is repairable today, but if I wait and it degenerates to the point that is *not* repairable in a year or two and thus needs to be replaced, this is not the best outcome. Wouldn't it be better to repair the valve now before it degenerates more and thus becomes non-repairable?"

The physician reminded me that open heart surgery is a serious procedure with risks. Perhaps he thought I seemed too eager to having the surgery. I pleaded with him to let me know how close I was to needing surgery based on blood leakage volume. He said that the only true way to measure the leakage and valve structure accurately is via a transesophageal echocardiogram (TEE), a minimally invasive procedure to measure the valve leakage by going through the lower esophagus versus the outer rib cage. He agreed to do this test, and it was scheduled for May 10, 2017, on an outpatient basis with a cardiologist colleague. After the procedure, as I was becoming conscious, the physician said, "Well, young man, you are going to see the surgeon. Your leakage is in fact at a severe level." I was immediately scheduled to see a cardiothoracic surgeon on May 23 for a surgical consult.

I am grateful that the Holy Spirit nudged me to seek a second opinion from Mayo. I knew there was something physically wrong with me, but I didn't know what course to take until directed by the Holy Spirit.

As I was driving home to Tucson knowing I would need surgery, I began to contemplate how I would tell my family. What did I need to do to prepare for this? It was a long two hours in the car. Once again, contemplative and asking for divine guidance, I heard that inner voice say to me, "Paul, read the New Testament in its entirety along with Psalms and Proverbs prior to surgery and highlight the sections I will show you."

This was a specific directive in my soul. I truly felt a presence instructing me to read the Bible—God's word to humanity. As an individual who believes in God, had accepted Jesus as God's Son and my personal redeemer, I now was determined to do exactly what I was moved to do. I literally began reading the New Testament along with the Psalms and Proverbs cover to cover as soon as possible! I have read the complete Bible many times during my life, but not in one sitting. I followed my conscience and began my journey into the Holy Word of God. My sister had given me a daily devotional Bible about thirty years ago. It has given me insight and helped me "stay the course" in this material world where the need to satisfy the self so easily takes exalted precedent over selfless stewardship toward others.

Perhaps I was at a crossroad in my life. Alternatively, I had just come up to a stop sign in my human life. Here I was, age fifty-eight, blessed with a great family, financially successful, and now I faced a serious heart condition that finally had caught up with me. Heart valves wear out. Mine was not normal, for whatever reason. It really didn't matter. I was headed for open heart surgery. I still felt in my soul that despite my defects, God the potter had wonderfully made me.

> *For thou didst form my inward parts, thou didst*
> *knit me together in my mother's womb. I praise thee,*
> *for thou art fearful and wonderful. Wonderful are*
> *thy works! Thou knoweth me right well.*
> *(Psalm 139:13–14)*

When I informed my family about the upcoming surgery, I asked them to pray for me. While waiting for the surgical consult appointment, I went back to being contemplative and seeking God's meaning in all this rapidly manifesting medical news. I simply returned to His Word, Holy Scripture. Reading the Bible has always brought comfort, peace, and wisdom to me in times of difficulty, pain, and life's challenges. The Bible has provided me with direction, meaning, purpose, and most importantly, hope—not only for tomorrow but for an eternal life with Jesus Christ. Hope is the cornerstone of faith. Hope and faith go hand in hand.

In preparation for the surgical consultation, I read the entire New Testament from May 11 through May 22.

Psalms and Proverbs would follow. As I read, I highlighted verses that impacted me. I knew I was ill and had no idea what my future held. Feelings of extreme anguish and the belief that something tragic was going to happen overwhelmed me.

May 23 came, and it was time to visit the surgeon. I kept praying that my mitral valve would be repairable as opposed to having it replaced. When my wife and I met with the surgeon, he informed us that he had studied my diagnostic heart tests and based on what he could see, he believed he had an 80 percent chance of repairing the existing mitral valve. The noninvasive approach was not an option, however; he needed to perform a full sternotomy so he could "see" the entire heart/valve structure. He also said very matter of factly that if he could not repair the valve, he would have to replace it, and he recommended the use of a mechanical valve. Finally, he added that due to his schedule, the earliest he could perform the procedure was mid-June.

This was a lot for us to digest all at once. For some reason I asked if there was any way he could perform the surgery sooner. I don't know why I asked him this. Who wants surgery earlier?

He left the exam room to check his schedule. He came back and said, "I can do it on Friday, June 2, at 7:30 a.m." He delivered the news efficiently, effectively, and directly. Without hesitation, I blurted out, "May I pray for you?" He said, "Sure." His physician's assistant, Maggie McClain, was in the room with us, and she seemed appreciative for us to be praying together. I knew she was a Christian by her enthusiastic buy in. I bowed my head and said, "Dear Lord, you brought me here today to this man of healing. Please, Lord, grant this physician the patience and precision to repair the valve you gave me so that replacing it will not be necessary. In the name of Jesus Christ, we pray. Amen." It was a direct, simple, and concise prayer.

The surgeon asked me to come back to Mayo on Friday, May 26, for an angiogram. He wanted to ensure that there were no blockages or other heart issues to attend to other than the valve prior to the operation. As he was getting ready to leave, I asked him if he could do me a favor while in the operating room. I showed him my upper exterior right thigh. I explained to him that I had been on a blood thinner for over a month and had an angiolipoma on the upper right side of my leg. The blood thinner had caused the capillaries to burst, and I was bleeding under the skin. Most of my thigh was purple and blue. I asked the surgeon if he could use his cauterization instrument and remove this while I was under anesthesia.

He responded, "I am a heart surgeon; we can deal with that at a later time." Even Beth seemed a little incredulous that I would ask a cardiac surgeon to remove a lipoma. At the time we did not know that the removal of the lipoma would in fact happen and prove to be a blessing in the near future.

When I had the angiogram, my heart had no blockages whatsoever. The medical staff told me to take it easy for the next week. Facing open heart surgery in seven days makes time precious. You begin to think about all the people you wish to contact and the things one needs to do. Facing my own mortality was the greatest wake-up call I could receive. Time did in fact become of great value. I had no control over my situation whatsoever. Knowing open heart surgery had risks, I spent most of the time between May 23 and June 1 reading the Bible, attempting to mentally prepare for my surgery. I found peaceful comfort in God's Word, yet I kept having feelings of distress, sorrow, and anguish of soul. I felt that something troubling was about to happen to me. I didn't fear death per se, but my spirit sensed that I was about to endure suffering. I often cried while reading the Bible. I began to send emails and messages to my wife and sons with devotional pages from my Bible along with the verses the Spirit directed me to highlight.

I did not share with my family my innermost feelings, but they commented that I appeared anxious and worrisome. It was much deeper than this, however. My soul literally felt that suffering awaited me. Day by day went by. I would weep miserably while reading the Bible. I did not understand at the time that the peace, comfort, and direction I had received from scripture in the past had somehow become an awakening of what life was truly all about. Namely, it was about my soul and how the soul longs to be with its Creator. Yet I kept feeling this uneasiness within me that I was going to suffer considerably. Not ever having these sensations before, I began to conclude that I might in fact die as a result of the surgery. Most of the biblical highlighting I did dealt with repentance, suffering, and death. At the same time, my highlights also included Scripture dealing with God's faithfulness, the promise of redemption and salvation for those who accept His Son, Jesus Christ. I was mentally going between utter despair and eternal hope continually. It was emotionally exhausting. I decided to accept God's divine will for whatever the outcome was to be. I was very concerned about my family, but I continued to keep these feelings to myself. In retrospect, and as you read further, I wish I had shared with them all of these feelings. But then again, this was my cross to bear. I desperately needed Christ to help me bear what I somehow knew was forthcoming.

On Sunday, May 28, 2017, Beth and I went to Mass at St. Mark's. I thanked God for all my blessings, reconfirmed my belief and acceptance of Jesus as my personal savior, and expressed humble gratitude for a wonderful life. I prayed for my wife, our sons and daughters-in-law, and our two grandchildren, Lorenzo and Gianna. Knowing we had a third grandchild on the way in July, I prayed that I would live to see Hannah, another gift from God. During the Mass, I stared at the crucifix above the altar and wondered how Jesus could bear the physical and emotional suffering unto death as a human being. He knew He would have to suffer to redeem mankind, and He selflessly gave himself for our salvation. To think that He did this for me, a sinner, and for all mankind is incomprehensible to the nonbeliever. To me it's factual truth.

"For God so loved the world that he gave his only Son, that whoever believes in him should not perish but have eternal life." (John 3:16)

I began to cry several times during Mass. My soul was full of sorrow despite knowing that God and Jesus loved me. I felt that soon I would face my own trial of suffering. After Mass I went over to the statue of the Precious Heart of Jesus (where his heart is visible outside his garments) and touched his heart on the statue and prayed for strength for my upcoming surgery. I prayed for His help and reaffirmed my faith in Him. I humbly accepted His will for my future.

After Mass Beth and I were home alone. At about 2:30 p.m., I heard a voice saying to me, "Go for a ride in the car now—alone." I informed Beth that I was going for a ride in the car and would be back shortly. She asked, "Where are you going?" and I answered, "I don't know."

Upon leaving my neighborhood, I asked, "Where am I to go?" The voice said, "Go to the base of the mountains," which was about a twenty-minute drive. As I proceeded to drive toward the mountain range, I approached an intersection that would require me to go right or left. I normally would go right, as this was the turning point to go back to our home. When I got to the intersection, the voice said to me, "Go left, and go to Santa Catalina Church."

Over the course of my life, I had driven by this church hundreds of times and had never even pulled into the parking lot. Not this day. I followed the instructions, pulled into the parking lot, got out of my car, and went to the church doors. I found them locked. I vividly remember saying to myself, "Why am I here, Lord? Why am I standing in front of a locked church?"

As I glanced to the right of the church, I saw a Mary,

Mother of Life prayer area. I went there and prayed. As I was leaving, I noticed that connected to this area was a walking path that led to an outdoor Stations of the Cross. I took a prayer pamphlet from the stand and proceeded to walk the path, praying at each station. When I got to the stations where Jesus fell, I had an incredible feeling in my soul of severe misery and suffering to the point of painful despair. I touched the Jesus statue of the stations and thought, *How could God allow His Son to suffer like this? The beatings, the scourging, the pain, the loss of blood . . . Why didn't God simply stop it and show all mankind that He is God? Then perhaps all mankind would believe and live according to His laws and teachings!*

My inner voice, the Holy Spirit, told me, "I came in human form to reconcile man to myself and open the kingdom of heaven to all who choose to believe in Me and My beloved Son." The voice also said, "Paul, you too are about to suffer, but I will be with you." I wept profusely. Knowing Christ suffered for me was comforting, but I did not want to die. However, I sensed that death might be near.

As I finished walking all the Stations of the Cross, I noticed another garden area with statutes. I walked over to examine what these figurines were. It was the Garden of Gethsemane with the disciples sleeping and Jesus alone weeping as he prayed for the cup to be taken from Him but that not His will be done but the will of God who sent Him. For the reader who may not know the final days of Christ's life or the story of His appeal to God to avert His crucifixion, the Garden of Gethsemane is specifically described in the Gospel of Matthew.

Then Jesus went with them to a place called Gethsemane, and said to His disciples, "Sit here while I go yonder and pray." And taking with him Peter and the two sons of Zebedee, he began to be sorrowed and troubled. Then he said to them, "My soul is very sorrowful, even to death; remain here and watch with Me." And going a little farther, he fell on his face and prayed, "My Father, if it is possible, let this cup pass from me; nevertheless, not as I will, but as thou wilt." And He came to the disciples and found them sleeping, and he said to Peter, "So, could you not watch with me one hour? Watch and pray that you may not enter into temptation; the spirit is indeed willing, but the flesh is weak." Again, for the second time, he went away and prayed, saying, "My Father, if this cannot pass unless I drink it, thy will be done." And again he came and found them sleeping, for their eyes were heavy. So, leaving them again, he went away and prayed for the third time, saying the same words. Then he came to the disciples and said to them, "Are you still sleeping and taking your rest? Behold, the hour is at hand, and the Son of Man is betrayed into the hands of sinners. Rise, let us be going; see my betrayer is at hand." (Matthew 26:36–46)

Jesus knew what was going to occur and that his mission on earth in human form was near completion. I too prayed for my own cup to be taken from me, but I acknowledged that I would accept His will concerning my life. I told Jesus I believed and trusted in Him. At this point, I again felt uncontrollable sorrow and anguish. I sensed the Holy Spirit saying, "You will suffer as well, Paul, but I am with you." Humanly, I honestly didn't know what this meant. I sensed I was being somehow foretold that an imminent event would occur as part of the surgery and that I might die.

My faith in Jesus Christ as my personal Savior was strong, but I wondered if it was strong enough to withstand all these premonitions of suffering and grief. Emotions are powerful forces. They can either lead you to sound reasoning or madness. For some reason, I had been directed to be at the Stations of the Cross and the garden alone that Sunday. I was reminded that Christ also wished for God to intervene yet yielded to His will. Mentally, I decided to do the same. Whatever was going to happen to me, it would be His will, not mine. I received a sense of peace in yielding myself this way.

As I was leaving the desert garden area, I noticed a sign saying that the entire display had just been created a month earlier in April 2017. I did not understand at the time that I was called there that day for a reason. I was being prepared for what would soon occur. Even though I trusted God's will for my being, it was incredibly difficult to completely surrender to my Creator.

I drove home, knowing I had experienced a very intimate conversation with God. There was not much more to do other than keep praying and waiting to be operated upon. Reasoning that I did not control the outcome of the surgery nor understanding what specifically lie ahead for me, I tried to let go and not dwell on the uncertainties I was facing.

Upon returning home, our son David was in the kitchen with Beth. They immediately inquired where I went, why I was gone so long, and expressed their concern for me. I shared with them that I had gone for a ride and decided to visit Santa Catalina Church, but I left out any details of the experiences that had transpired. Some things are best left between God and yourself.

In the days leading up to surgery, I began to pray more diligently with a grateful heart. My prayers were no longer focused on myself, as I knew I was saved if I died. I searched deep in my heart about what was truly important for me to implore God to do. I tried desperately to cling to hope, yet I understood that God takes each of us when He decides. So, rather than dwell on myself, I made two specific requests of God.

My first petition was that my entire immediate family would witness God's love and the Holy Spirit's power in whatever His will would be relative to my surgery. Specifically, no matter what happened to me, I asked the Lord to ensure that my family's souls were saved and their faith would grow. I wanted to be an example to trust in God always. This petition was for my entire immediate family: my wife, Beth; our sons, Michael and David; our daughters-in-law, Tara and Jonna; my brother, Steve, and his girlfriend, Diane; my sister, Donna, and her husband, Eric; my nephew, Steven; and our grandchildren, Lorenzo, Gianna, and soon-to-be-born Hannah. More specifically I asked that each of them not only come to know Christ but accept Him as their personal Savior. I also asked the Lord to bless them and protect them.

My second petition was that whatever suffering that awaited me, I would use it to evangelize all I encountered in the name of Jesus. I know you can't negotiate with God; however, I asked Him that if I survived, He would use me to add souls to His kingdom while I was still alive on earth. I wanted to be a messenger of His grace, love, and mercy, a living example.

Honestly, I did have a third, selfish prayer request. It was that I would survive the surgery and live to see all my children's children (grandchildren) and great grandchildren. I drew upon my mother's similar requests while she was ill with cancer some thirty-five years earlier.

I prayed constantly while I finished reading the Bible the week of surgery. I reached out to many Christian people I knew throughout the country and asked them to pray for me. I also kept asking my family to pray for me. I had a strong sense in my soul that something was going to happen to me.

My beloved wife went to a Christian store and purchased a crucifix on a chain for me to bring with me to the hospital. A woman's intuition is real. She sensed my anxiety and pensiveness and witnessed my tears continually as I read the Bible. She presented me with the cross as a constant reminder that Christ is with me and had promised me salvation. Little did I know that this gift would become not only symbolic but something I would clutch tightly in the very near future. God knew I was going to need this for strengthening my hope. Thank you, Beth, for the gift of the cross!

One evening during the week prior to surgery, I was lying in bed, ready to fall asleep. My wife was also in bed. I suddenly felt the lower part of the corner of the bed adjacent to my feet sink as if someone had just sat down at the foot of the bed. I was wide awake and it felt so real! I immediately asked Beth if the dog was on the bed. She said no, so I turned on the light, but no one was there. Beth suggested that perhaps it was my guardian angel preparing me for what would lie ahead.

The next day I downloaded many Christian songs on my iPad for use while in the hospital. This was a first for me; I had never put a library of Christian songs together. Again, I felt I was being prepared by someone much larger than my mind could comprehend. I called Fr. John Arnold, our pastor at St. Mark's, and asked him if I could receive the sacrament of the sick.

For those non-Catholic readers, the anointing of the sick is one of seven sacraments in the Catholic Church. It is administered to a Catholic who, having reached the age of reason, begins to be in danger due to sickness or old age. A priest places the palms of his hands on the sick person's head, using holy oil blessed by the bishop.

Fr. Arnold asked if I could come to 8:00 a.m. Mass on June 1, 2017. He administered the sacrament after Mass and asked those present to perform the laying on of the hands. I sobbed miserably during the anointing as my being was very troubled about what was to occur. I couldn't rid myself of the sense of impending affliction, suffering or death itself. Simply said, my soul was grieving and troubled.

After I got home from church, I began to pack my hospital overnight bag. We had planned to drive to Phoenix that afternoon since I had to be in the pre-operating area by 5:30 a.m. the next day. As I was getting ready, I went into my home office. I opened the Bible and began to write out by hand several verses that had touched me. I also pulled out my personal mission statement, reflected on the younger me who wrote it, and read it again. I noted that my date of birth was clearly typed as April 15, 1959. Next to this was the line "Date of Death_____. I began to cry. I picked up a pen and began to write June 2, 2017, as the date of my death. That's how much anguish I felt about the surgery the next day. Weeping, I stopped the pen an inch from the paper as I began to complete the line. I ceased by telling myself that my date of death is not for me to discern—that once again it was God's will, not mine. I recall thinking at that pivotal moment, *He is the potter; you are the clay.* I prayed that he would not discard me, but instead remake me.

I then made a handwritten note on my personal mission statement that said, "Please give to my children and grandchildren." I guess I was trying to leave a roadmap for our sons and grandchildren in the event I was to die. I wanted them to know who their father and grandfather was as a person. I left this facedown on my desk for someone to find if I passed.

Little did I know at the time the foreboding of my

spirit's messaging. I truly felt compelled to write the date of death on my mission statement. Then I felt that perhaps this was to be completed by someone else other than me. I then fervently copied the various Scripture verses I thought important for my loved ones, especially our sons. I made a copy for each son, again placing them facedown on my desk for someone to find. I looked around and thought, "This may be the last time you leave this house." I remember also thinking what a blessed life I had had.

Finally, I reviewed some last-minute emails. One was from Dynamic Catholic about available books. I paused at length and read this email in detail. Then I ordered three books randomly with enough copies for my family. The books were *The One Thing* by Matthew Kelly, *Mission of the Family* by Jon Leonetti, and *Nine Words* by Allen Hunt. I thought I would read them and give copies to each family member after my discharge. I guess it was my way of providing myself with hope for the future, and the books would be a gift to my family.

Beth and I headed to Phoenix; my brother, Steve, and his girlfriend, Diane, drove from Prescott to Phoenix that afternoon as well. We planned to have an early dinner together that night. Steve had been struck by a car while riding his bicycle in 2000, and as a result of the accident, he is a paraplegic. He is a testament to courageous strength and perseverance. Meanwhile, my younger sister, Donna—one of the most devout Christians I know—initially was not going to drive up from Tucson for my surgery. I specifically called her to request that she be with me because she is a true believer and I know her prayers are heard due to her tremendous faith. Donna and her husband, Eric, honored my request and drove to Mayo early the morning of my surgery.

Little did I know at the time how much they were supposed to be there. But God knew. I had faith and hope, but did I really trust God's will for me?

CHAPTER FOUR

GOD SPEAKS TO MY SOUL—TRIALS AND SUFFERINGS AWAIT

*Have no anxiety about anything, but in everything by prayer and
supplication with thanksgiving let your requests be made known to God.
And the peace of God, which passes all understanding, will keep your
hearts and your minds in Christ Jesus.*
PHILIPPIANS 4:6–7

Beth and I went to bed early the evening before the surgery. I prayed for God through his Son Jesus Christ to forgive my sins. I reiterated that I accepted His will for me regardless of the surgical outcome. I also kept reflecting on the potter and the clay Scriptures. It was an analogy I could wrap my brain around. I vividly remember praying to God, "You are the potter; I am merely the clay. Please do not throw this pot into the fire as no longer useful. Rather, Lord, restore this pot of clay and use it for your glory and purposes."

I slept peacefully. Arising at 4:45 a.m., I showered and got dressed. Other than personal clothing, I brought three items with me to the hospital that morning; my Bible, the crucifix necklace from Beth, and an iPad with my Christian music.

We entered the hospital and checked in at 5:30 a.m. I was called back about 5:50 a.m. for pre-operative preparation. I had my crucifix with me, and I asked if I could bring it into surgery. The staff said yes, but that it would be placed under my pillow during surgery. I thought about what a blessed life I had enjoyed. Always planning, always praying, always focused on family and trying to serve others. And now I found myself completely dependent on others. I became anxious and just wanted "this" to be over with—whatever "this" was to be. I asked that God would direct the surgeon and his team to have a successful repair of my mitral valve.

As I was being prepped for surgery, talking to God from my inner being, the nurse interrupted me and asked about the purple bruising on the right side of my thigh. I told her that since they put me on blood thinners, I had a painful angiolipoma that was bleeding out under my skin. She said to the staff, "Please, let's note this with the surgeon, as the patient will continue on blood thinners post operatively." As I would find out later, this too was yet another blessing in disguise. God does take care of details.

After my prep, they allowed my family to come in to wish me well. I prayed with my family as all were there. I had memorized a Scripture passage from the Apostle Paul's epistle to the Romans that had deep meaning for me, as it spoke to life's journey, its trials, and the hope we cling to. It also speaks to God's love being placed in our heart and the power of the Holy Spirit. This passage had it all as far as I was concerned, and I shared it with my family:

More than that, we rejoice in our sufferings,
knowing that suffering produces endurance, and
endurance produces character and character produces
hope, and hope does not disappoint us, because God's
love has been poured into our hearts through the Holy
Spirit who has been given to us. (Romans 5:3–5)

From my perspective, this verse tells me that we suffer during this earthly life, yet we continue onward. Those who can't get through suffering become victims to their circumstances. Those who turn suffering into inner strength build upon their mental and moral qualities as individuals. Then, realizing we are mere mortal beings, we must hope in the promise of eternal life as committed to us by Jesus Christ. Thus, hope will never disappoint because God is love and he unconditionally loves us and has given each of us his Holy Spirit of truth which resides in our souls.

Several Mayo medical staff prayed as well with our family. It provided additional comfort knowing faithful people would be caring for me. I said a tearful good-bye to my family and proceeded to surgery.

The next thing I remember was hearing the surgeon's voice in my ear saying, "It took us five hours, but I got the valve repaired; you're good to go. I will see you later." My breathing tube was removed, and I said hello to my family. Donna said that my first words to her once conscious were, "It's time to evangelize." I was transferred to the ICU floor to recover. It seemed that everything had gone well, and I would be discharged from the hospital in approximately five days. Other than being a little groggy from surgery, I felt okay. I cherished that I was alive and conversing with my family. I also noticed a bandaged incision on the side of my right thigh. The cardiac surgeon did in fact remove the lipoma during the procedure.

The next day Beth and our son David left the hospital campus to go to lunch. Meanwhile, my sister, Donna, had just returned from lunch and was conversing with me in my room. The nurse had just visited and left the room. At 2:10 p.m. I had my first cardiac arrest. This means your heart stops beating normally and you will die quickly without an intervention. I guess life does change in the blink of an eye. I never heard "code blue" or any sounds whatsoever from machines or the Mayo personnel. I was just gone.

What occurred next was revelatory. I literally could see the medical professionals all around me working on my lifeless body. It was totally silent, and I recognized the body as mine, but in a strange way I had no concern about anything. In this silence, I saw one person performing CPR on me. Not hearing anything, I remember wondering why they were doing this to me. I also had no concept of time, which I have now learned is critical when one is in cardiac arrest. Without blood flow, the brain usually begins to die within three to four minutes.

The next thing that happened was that I left the hospital room as a brilliant white light appeared and attracted me toward itself, similar to being pulled into its presence. I was traveling rapidly into the light. There was blue around the light, like the color of the sky. As I was progressing into this light, it seemed as though I was being drawn both toward and into it. The light was the most pure white in color, and it felt penetrating. It was not at all blinding like sunlight, but rather a pure, brilliant white. As I progressed into the radiant light, the blue disappeared, and it became very still. I was completely in the presence of this beautiful light. The light enveloped me and surrounded me. I cannot adequately explain what I experienced using human terms.

While traveling into the light, I thought, *What is this and where am I going?* When it enveloped me, I felt like I was home. The adjectives to describe these feelings in common language would be unconditional love, joy, peace, beauty, and happiness all rolled into one. Once these attributes took over my being, I recall thinking, *I did die; I am in heaven. Thank you, God, thank you.* I felt I was home where I belonged. As there was no concept of time, I don't know how long I was there, nor how long my spirit traveled into the light.

Then I was somehow back in my body. I could hear my heart beating in my chest and all the medical machines sounding. I could hear the medical staff talking with one another and shouting instructions. I didn't understand what was going on. Then a doctor above my head looked straight down at me and said, "Paul, say something."

I replied, "You used 150 joules on me didn't you, Doctor?"

He looked at his colleagues and said, "Who is this guy? How does he know how many joules we gave him?" I didn't know this physician at the time. His name was

Dr. Jonathan McGarvey, and fate would have us meet again in about three weeks. God brings people into our lives for a reason. I believe the reason is to demonstrate His continual presence in our lives and the lives of all.

Not even knowing I had a cardiac arrest, the next thing I remember after being revived was the original surgeon's voice again whispering in my ear, "What happened was an anomaly. You are fine. The valve repair is fine; we're all good—you're okay." I nodded yes, even though I still did not understand what he was talking about. No one ever used the term *cardiac arrest* in my hearing. So I didn't understand at the time what had occurred clinically to me.

I rested late Saturday and slept well that night. Early Sunday morning, they drew blood and asked me to stand next to my bed and march in place. I complied. I got back in bed, and at about 9:00 a.m., the cardiac arrests started again.

CHAPTER FIVE

LIFE IN THE BALANCE—JESUS, MY REDEEMER

Jesus looked at them and said, "With men this is impossible, but with God all things are possible."
MATTHEW 19:26

It was Pentecost Sunday, June 4, 2017. I wasn't aware of this fact while lying in an ICU trying to recover from open heart surgery. However, it would become the day that the love and mercy of God would manifest itself through the power of the Holy Spirit to intervene for me. The Feast of Pentecost is celebrated on the fiftieth day after Easter, the day Christ rose from the dead so we could be redeemed. When Jesus foretold of his impending death, he advised his disciples to remain in Jerusalem until the Holy Spirit was placed upon them. Pentecost commemorates the descent of the Holy Spirit upon the Apostles while they were celebrating the Jewish Feast of Weeks. The Holy Spirit appeared as tongues of fire over them, and they all spoke different languages yet understood one another. This event represents the birth of the Church to many Christians as the Apostles traveled to many parts of the world and had to know the native language in order to evangelize and build Christ's church. Of all days for me to start dying again, the Holy Day of Pentecost was prophetic.

My cardiac arrests started at about 9:00 a.m. that morning. The Mayo team would use defibrillators continually until my normal heart beat returned. Then I would have another cardiac arrest. More shocking, followed by another cardiac arrest. It must have been horrific for my wife and family to witness. My entire family was there except our son Michael, who was at home with his family about fifteen miles from the hospital. Beth called him to inform him that I was coding regularly and to get to the hospital immediately. Michael rushed to Mayo, came into my room, and stood by the head of my bed. He said, "Dad, its Mike. I'm here." Upon hearing this, I looked at Michael and immediately had another cardiac arrest spontaneously right before his eyes. Remember, to this point in time, no one had used the word cardiac arrest in ear shot of me. I had no idea what was happening to me.

The Mayo team kept using the paddles to restore my heart rhythm. Again and again I would have another cardiac arrest. This went on for almost two hours. The ICU physician informed my family that they weren't sure why this was occurring, but that they were going to cease defibrillation; it was inhumane to keep paddling a person this way. Treatment was ending, and hope for survival fading. The chaplain was present, and many were praying for me, including the families of other patients in the ICU. Thank God! How many "Code Blue Room 20" would a family have to hear and deal with emotionally? I never heard code blue at all from my dying world.

At about 10:45 a.m., the doctors convened the family together. Dr. Srivathsan, the department head of cardiac electrophysiology at Mayo, was there, along with the ICU team. They shared with Beth that they did not understand why the cardiac arrests were occurring, but they asked her to sign a consent form for the physicians to perform an emergent angiogram to rule out a blood clot from surgery or from all the shocking of the paddles. They also asked her if lifesaving procedures or measures were okay to perform. Beth naturally consented. I was reaching the end of my earthly life.

During this critical time, I had no clue what was happening to me. Either I was unconscious or heavily sedated, or both. I would have eight cardiac arrests requiring defibrillator resuscitation on Pentecost Sunday morning.

"Because he cleaves to me in love, I will deliver him; I will protect him, because he knows my name. When he calls to me, I will answer him; I will be with him in trouble, I will rescue him and honor him. With long life I will satisfy him, and show him my salvation." (Psalm 91: 14–16)

While I was being transported for the emergent angiogram, Michael told Beth and his brother David that he was leaving the hospital. Beth shared later that Michael was visibly distressed, and she was very concerned about him. Where was he going at this cataclysmic time? Michael took my crucifix from my hospital room and told the family he was going to church! No one knew he had taken the crucifix from my bedside. He left, not knowing if he would ever see his father alive again. Our youngest son David would assume the role and responsibility of the remaining man in the family and was left to comfort his mother. David and Beth clung to one another. As Michael approached his car in the Mayo parking lot, he Googled the nearest Catholic Church. He saw that St. Bernadette's was only a few miles away. He also saw St. Paul's come up. He sensed that he wanted to go to St. Paul's given it was my name. He initially disregarded this "sense" and went to St. Bernadette's as he thought time was of the essence. Michael went to the front doors of the church, only to discover them being locked; the services were over. A parishioner gave him the digital code to gain access to the chapel so he could go there to pray.

Michael prayed for about a half hour. While he and others prayed, the angiogram was performed and no clots or blockages were found. Meanwhile at Mayo, Dr. Srivathsan oversaw a lifesaving procedure given there was no blood clot or blockage. He tried to give me time to rest. They performed a left stellate ganglion block procedure. In layman's terms, they anesthetize the nerve from the brain that controls breathing and heartbeat as part of one's autonomous function. When they shut off the nerve, heartbeat and breathing cease. They then use an electronic temporary pacemaker along with a ventilator to mechanically keep the patient alive by having the machines beat the heart and breathe for them. Thank God for technology. Essentially I was on full life support with heavy sedation. I reappeared in the ICU unconscious, on life support, and with something sticking out of my neck—another difficult sight for my family. The doctors informed my family that I was to rest for at least a day.

As Michael was about to leave the chapel at St. Bernadette's to come back to Mayo, David called to check on him and informed him that I was back in ICU and alive, although intubated again. He told his older brother to take his time getting back and that he was taking care of Mom. God's timing is amazing. If David had not called his brother at that time, Michael would have simply returned to the hospital with my crucifix. However, after receiving the call from David, Michael decided to drive in the opposite direction toward St. Paul's Church. He sensed he should have gone there all along. Now with the encouragement from his brother, he continued to St. Paul's since he knew there was nothing he could do for me at the hospital. God was directing him there.

Michael entered St. Paul's toward the end of the Sunday Mass. He noticed there was a first Communion ceremony being conducted. He received Communion, and then exited the church and sat in the Stations of the Cross garden at St. Paul's, waiting for the patrons to leave after the celebration. He did not know that I too had been in a Stations of the Cross garden exactly a week earlier in Tucson. He wanted to wait and then go back into the church and speak to the priest. Michael had no idea who he was about to encounter.

CHAPTER SIX

GOD'S INTERVENTION—
THE POWER OF THE HOLY SPIRIT

If the spirit of him who raised Jesus from the dead dwells in you, he who raised Christ Jesus from the dead will give life to your mortal bodies also, through his Spirit who dwells in you.
ROMANS 8:11

When Michael reentered the church, he sat toward the back. Upon seeing someone accompanying the clergy, he asked if he could speak to the priest because his father was critically ill. The stranger politely informed Michael that the person was not the priest; it was the Bishop of Phoenix, the Most Reverend Thomas J. Olmsted. Michael quickly apologized, and the bishop's emissary told Michael to wait in the pew and he would go see the bishop. After a few minutes, Bishop Olmsted appeared and greeted our son. Michael immediately shared with Bishop Olmsted what was happening with me. He showed him the crucifix he had taken from my hospital room. Bishop Olmsted comforted Michael, and they prayed together—one man praying for his earthly father, the other for a complete stranger some eleven miles away in the ICU on life support whose heart and lungs are working via machinery. With my ganglion nerve anesthetized, my heart and lungs could not biologically function. Michael had no idea of my clinical state.

"For where two or three are gathered together
in my name, there I am in the midst of them."
(Matthew 18:20)

Michael thanked Bishop Olmsted for his time and prayers. Michael later told us that after praying with the bishop, he had received a complete sense of peace in his soul. Regardless of what was going to occur to me, he was at peace. He had given it all to God.

Michael ended up at St. Paul's for a reason. He had wanted to go there initially but was torn about being gone that long from the Mayo ICU and family. God intervened by having David call him as he was about to come back to the hospital. Our family believes the Holy Spirit directed Michael to be where he needed to be and when he needed to be there. This was obviously a preordained path for him.

Is anyone among you sick? Let him call for the elders
of the church, and let them pray over him, anointing
him with oil in the name of the Lord; and the
prayer of faith will save the sick man, and the Lord
will raise him up; and if he has committed sins, he
will be forgiven. Therefore, confess your sins to one
another, and pray for one another, so that you may
be healed. The prayer of a righteous man has great
power in its effects. (James 5:14–16)

Personally, I don't believe there are any "coincidences" in life. The Master has a plan for each and every one of us. The definition of the word *coincidence* is "a remarkable concurrence of events or circumstances without apparent casual connection." Having my son meet the Bishop of Phoenix at St. Paul's Church on Pentecost Sunday, June 4, 2017, is nothing less than miraculous. Maricopa County in Arizona is 9,224 square miles in size and has a population of 4.2 million people. What are the odds of these two individuals meeting and praying for me? At such a specific place as St. Paul's Catholic Church at that specific time? Miracles do happen.

"It is the Spirit that gives life; the flesh is of no avail; the words that I have spoken to you are spirit and life." (John 6:63)

Bishop Olmsted would later share with me that not only did he pray for me with my son at St. Paul's, but that upon returning home he entered his chapel and continued to pray for me Sunday afternoon. He was moved by Michael's faith in seeking God's intervention. The Holy Spirit unequivocally intervened in my medical distress using this remarkable, godly man.

Meanwhile, back at Mayo, I lay in the ICU heavily sedated with ventilator support. Michael returned and placed my crucifix next to my bed. My family continued to pray and soft Christian music played in the background. Beth slept in the chair adjacent to my bed Sunday evening. Prayer, prayer and more prayer. Thank you, Jesus!

59

Jesus said, "Therefore I tell you, whatever you ask in prayer, believe that you have received it and it will be yours." (Mark 11:24)

On Monday, I awoke. I had no idea what day it was. It was as if Sunday had never existed. When I gained consciousness, I immediately noticed I was on a ventilator, unable to communicate. I saw everyone at the foot of my bed and wondered what was going on. I became frightened as no one wanted to tell me anything and risk upsetting me. However, by their facial expressions I sensed something had gone wrong. Even now, I never heard the words *cardiac arrest* nor ever felt them physically.

I reached for people's hands and tried to write letters slowly in the palms of their hands in order to make words and thus try to communicate. Our daughter-in-law Jonna was able to readily decipher my alphabet finger spelling on her hand. She became my interpreter. The doctors removed me from the ventilator at midday. I felt dazed, confused, and tired. My family urged me to rest. I listened to Christian music all day, still unaware of what I had been through. I talked to God a lot that day. I constantly thanked Jesus for being my Savior, reaffirmed my faith in Him, and petitioned the Holy Spirit and the heavenly hosts to help me. Somehow in the depths of my despair, I knew that God's love for me was constant and infinite. I kept dwelling on the experience of going into the light and feeling His presence. I focused on where I went in Spirit, and I desperately wanted to share it with others. I had a sense of equanimity that I could not explain.

Late that day, the nurse asked me if I could get out of bed and stand. I tried to comply, but my knees buckled and I was too weak to stand on my own. It was back to bed for Monday night. With Beth in the chair next to me, we reminded each other of our love for one another and our wonderful family. I had the crucifix she gave me in my right hand with the chain wrapped around my wrist. I shared with my family and the nurses what I had witnessed and where I had been. Being able to share the experience was joyful and cathartic for me.

On Tuesday, I awoke and remembered to wish my sister Donna a very happy birthday. My family and the clinical staff at Mayo hadn't shared any details of what had happened over the weekend. I honestly didn't know what had actually transpired. Early Tuesday morning, a physician came into my room. He introduced himself to me as Dr. Srivathsan and informed me that I had had eight cardiac arrests and he wanted to fit me with a cardiac life vest for sixty days. After that I would come back to the hospital to have an implantable device placed in my chest. That was it. It was the first time I heard the news straight from the source.

Dr. Srivathsan shared what had happened to me but without any explanation as to why it occurred. I was numb. I was finally coherent, and I got the news of my medical ordeal with no rationale as to what happened, how it happened, or why it happened. I thought, *Okay,*

I'm alive, and God has me exactly where He wants me.
I thought about the light I had gone into. It gave me consolation and comfort.

A few hours later, the valve repair surgeon came in to my room and asked how I was feeling and whether Dr. Srivathsan had been in with a "game plan." I shared with him the life vest conversation, and he said he would confer with Dr. Srivathsan about the next steps. The Mayo team conferred and the game plan changed. Dr. Srivathsan shared that they would be scheduling me for a procedure to implant a permanent pacemaker and ICD. When I heard the need for an additional surgery, reality quickly sank in. I had almost died once on Saturday and eight times on Sunday. I glanced at my Bible on my hospital tray and clung to my crucifix in my right hand. I felt God was with me regardless. This was a new beginning for me. I actually asked myself, "Why am I still here?"

I visited with family most of Tuesday and told them again what I witnessed concerning leaving my body and going into an enveloping brilliant white light. Mayo personnel had me up and walking around the ICU, dragging my IV pole and cardiac monitor. They seemed surprised that I was alive, let alone walking. Several said it was so good to see me. As I passed some nurses on my brief walk, I heard one of them say, "That's the guy," probably meaning "That's the guy who had eight cardiac arrests." She was being polite.

I recall asking God for restored health while also simultaneously acknowledging that dying was acceptable too if it was His will. I still had hope, but I had given up fear and trying to control an unknown future. I was spiritually at peace despite being humanly concerned.

CHAPTER SEVEN

THE PARADOX OF LIFE VERSUS DEATH—
THE MESSAGE FROM A EUCHARISTIC
VISITOR

*For we know that if the earthly tent we live in is destroyed, we
have a building from God, a house not made with hands, eternal in
the heavens. Here indeed we groan, and long to put on our heavenly
dwelling, so that by putting it on we may not be found naked. For while
we are still in this tent, we sigh with anxiety, not that we would be
unclothed, but that we would be further clothed, so that what is mortal
may be swallowed up by life. He who has prepared us for this very
thing is God, who has given us the Spirit as a guarantee.
So we are always of good courage; we know that while we are at home
in the body we are away from the Lord, for we walk by faith, not by
sight. We are of good courage, and we would rather be away from the
body and at home with the Lord. So whether we are at home or away,
we make it our aim to please him. For we must all appear before the
judgment seat of Christ, so that each one may receive good or evil,
according to what he had done in the body.*
2 CORINTHIANS 5:1–10

Something else was going on within me. Although physically sore and hurting, I was mentally acutely alive. It is
hard to describe, but I will try. As I continued to grasp the
cross in my hand, I contemplated why God had allowed
me to live. I became devoid of physical issues or sensations and gave all my reasoning to my spiritual being. I

was searching for meaning beyond my bodily existence. Perhaps I was simply accepting that my body would die as it recently had done several times. My rational, finite mind was seeking an infinite God while simultaneously acknowledging that God cannot be understood by the human mind. Nonetheless, there was a tremendous comfort and peace even thinking about an all-knowing and loving God. Through contemplation, faith and hope were constant companions in my finite world. Prior to surgery, faith and hope were distinctively separate aspirations. Now they were somehow one and the same.

I kept dwelling on what I had seen and how I had felt in my "near-death experience." What I had seen spiritually— without any of my five senses—was amazingly beautiful. If I ever needed confirmation that God and the spiritual realm existed, I had found it—or better yet, it had found me. As I lay in the ICU, I processed my thoughts, trying to make sense of why all these things occurred and why my family had to witness all of it.

Beth and I have many friends and dear colleagues. Many of them were calling my cell phone, emailing and texting me, my wife, and our sons. Everyone wanted to know how I was doing. It had been four days since my surgery and our family had been silent to these requests for information. We conferred as a family and decided to tell close friends what had happened. We asked people to continue their prayers for my next procedure, which was scheduled for June 9, 2017.

I had one physical issue that I could not figure out rationally. Every time I closed my eyes, I saw red rather than black or darkness. Initially there was a fine mosaic pattern of fine black lines throughout the crimson red color. I couldn't help but think there was something wrong with me. Was it some sort of neurological damage due to the cardiac arrests? I refrained from sharing this with my family as I didn't want to upset them. Nor did I want to discuss this with the medical staff; I was just grateful to be alive.

Then Wednesday morning, a woman with a wooden cross around her neck walked into my hospital room while I was alone. She introduced herself as Estella, a Eucharistic Minister, from St. Bernadette's Catholic Church. She asked if I wanted the Eucharist, and I said yes. She gave me Communion and we prayed together. I shared with her my experience and the testimony of the light, and we both wept together as well. Before she left, she gave me the St. Bernadette church bulletin from Sunday, the day of my eight cardiac arrests. Alone again, I began to read the bulletin and noticed that Sunday, June 4, 2017, was Pentecost Sunday. The bulletin was full of beautiful Scripture references regarding the Holy Spirit and the meaning of Pentecost. I read that the symbolic color of the Holy Spirit is red, and on Pentecost the church is decorated in red. Pieces of the puzzle began to fall into place in my mind. The color red and its symbolism to the Holy Spirit was surreal to me. I now understood why I was seeing red. It meant that the Holy Spirit was within me. I instantly recalled Romans 5:5, the last verse of the prayer I had said before surgery. The dots connected again.

*And hope does not disappoint us, because God's love
has been poured into our hearts through the Holy
Spirit who has been given to us. (Romans 5:5)*

I now had peace and hope. My energy level increased,
and I reaffirmed my desire to share with others the message
of salvation through faith in Jesus. Estella had been used
by God to awaken me spiritually. I quickly grabbed the
Pentecost bulletin to look for the phone number. I called
St. Bernadette's, and a Mitzie answered the phone. I
thanked her immensely for having Estella come by. She
graciously offered to have Fr. Edward Gilbert come by too
since he was currently at Mayo as well.

Fr. Gilbert literally was in my hospital room within ten
minutes! My wife had returned to the room as well. Fr.
Gilbert prayed with us and we thanked him. I really felt
God's presence, and I felt comfort in my soul knowing
that I was in the Holy Spirit's care and love along with an
incredibly loving and supportive family. Being reminded
that the love of God had been poured out into my *heart*
through the *Holy Spirit* was of great comfort to me.

At this point in time I wasn't aware that Michael had
left the hospital and prayed with the bishop. My family
slowly began to share what had transpired in detail. The
events were interesting, to say the least. They told me how
I had eight cardiac arrest codes on Sunday in addition
to the one on Saturday. During the cardiac arrest on
Pentecost Sunday morning, they shared the traumatic
events and details.

As our entire family was talking about the details

68

with one another, I opened up about seeing the color red when I closed my eyes. I knew by faith that this was the Holy Spirit within me telling me that I was not alone. I had peace in my heart; I knew that God's will was all I needed. His unfailing love was my soul's guarantee. The Bible next to me, the crucifix in my hand, and a loving family—what more could I ask for?

I also told my family that it was okay if I should pass away unexpectedly. I knew where I was going, and I felt the Holy Spirit's presence. Michael then shared what he did on Sunday—how he ended up at St. Paul's with Bishop Olmsted because of the phone message from David. To say I was astonished is an understatement. I couldn't grasp this initially. Michael pointed to the bottom of the hospital television where he had printed and taped a verse:

I can do all things in him (Christ) who strengthens me. (Philippians 4:13)

That night Beth again stayed in my room, sleeping in the one and only chair. For the first time I thought about getting well physically. I had been saved by grace.

It was now Thursday, June 8. Dr. Srivathsan came into my room to confer with me about the procedure, which was scheduled for the following morning at 10:00 a.m. The normal way to do the procedure is to put a ventricular lead wire into the ventricular portion of the heart through the tricuspid valve. My tricuspid valve had some "leaflets," and he had concerns about doing anything inside my heart after the cardiac arrests. Dr. Srivathsan, who was also the department head, was the only surgeon who could feed the wire through a coronary sinus vein around the heart as an alternative. The shocking lead would then lie underneath the ventricle itself.

He was not sure this would be successful—it depended on the size and diameter of my veins once they were into the procedure. He said, "We will try and go through the coronary sinus vein, but if we can't, are you okay with going through the tricuspid valve?"

I thought for a moment, felt the Holy Spirit's presence and peace, and replied, "I believe you will be able to do this through the veins, but if you can't, use your best judgment." I began to pray for Dr. Srivathsan, asking the Lord to give him the ability to get the wires through the vein.

Shortly after Dr. Srivathsan left, I received a call on my cell phone from Fr. George Holley, the associate pastor at St. Mark Catholic Church, our home parish in Tucson. He had heard through Dick Johnson (another parishioner) that I had had some serious complications. Dick had been at Mayo the day before for his own appointment and had stopped by to visit me Wednesday afternoon. I told Fr. George about everything that had transpired, along with the upcoming procedure. We prayed together over the phone, and I asked him to continue to pray that Dr. Srivathsan would be able to utilize the vein to thread the wire. I also reached out to family and friends via email to pray for the same outcome. We again resorted to the power of prayer.

I encouraged my sons to read the Bible and strengthen their faith. It was early in the evening and I heard a voice in my head say, "Thank Michael for his actionable faith and prayers, for they were heard." Not understanding the message, I asked to speak to Michael alone. Rather than repeating what I just heard in my head, I instead asked him a series of open-ended questions. "Michael, why did you leave your mother and brother when the medical staff gave you all the news that treatment was ceasing and the chaplain was called? Why did you decide to go to church with my crucifix? What compelled you to do this?"

His response was without hesitation. He said, "Dad, I was desperate. I didn't know what else to do, so I turned to God and His Church."

I was amazed at this answer. I said, "Michael, the Church is the body of Christ. The Holy Spirit has told me to thank you for your actionable faith that led to prayers that were heard and answered. Thank you, son." I told Michael that it is easy to simply pray for someone. However, in his case he went beyond prayer and demonstrated faith in action. The fact that he took the crucifix with him was symbolically powerful. For him, it was all he could take of me. We revisited together all the miracles that occurred on Pentecost Sunday. We both pondered the fact that he eventually went to the church which was named St. Paul, with Bishop Olmsted presiding at that time, at that location on Pentecost Sunday. There are no coincidences. It was all part of God's plan. Oh, the power of prayer! We told each other how much we loved one another. I slept peacefully on Thursday evening, knowing I was in the loving hands of Jesus.

On Friday morning about 6:30 a.m., I was awakened by Maggie McClain, the initial surgeon's physician's assistant, entering my room. She looked exhausted. We said hello and I mentioned she looked really tired. She said she had just worked through the night due to some emergency surgeries and was going home, but she wanted to stop by and wish me well. I was amazed at her selflessness. She said that many people at the hospital were talking about what a miracle I was. She also said, "Paul, many people in medicine are scientific in nature and do not believe in the spiritual realm of health and healing. I am a Christian, so I believe everything you witnessed and have testified to during your cardiac arrests."

She went on to say, "I believe this happened to you in order to strengthen your faith and help others believe and thus be led to Christ." She encouraged me to write down everything and perhaps even write a book. I thanked her for her prayers and support. As you can tell, I followed her advice and wrote this book. She planted the seed; God watered it.

The ICU staff informed my family about 9:30 a.m. that they would have to leave my room so the ICU could be cleaned. They also stated that they were running behind in the Cath Lab and my procedure would tentatively occur about noon. So there I sat, alone all morning. Before I knew it, it was noon. By early afternoon, I was physically miserable without any food or water since the night before. Alone for about five hours, all I did was pray. I prayed that the Lords' will was for me to have a successful procedure and recover fully. I asked Jesus to use me as a living example for my immediate family to bring them closer to Christ and their individual salvation. I then continued petitioning God and Christ to help me evangelize and influence many other souls who choose to accept Christ as their personal savior and redeemer. My desire was the same as it had been all along: to lead my family and others to a deep relationship with Christ.

At 2:30 p.m. visitors were allowed again, and my wife came into my room. She excitedly pulled out a St. Anthony (the patron saint of miracles) prayer card that was sealed in its original cellophane package. On the back was a decade of the rosary. Beth explained that our daughter-in-law Tara's mother found the card that morning on the living room floor next to our four-year-old grandson Lorenzo's toys. Tara said she had cleaned the house the day before, but she had never seen the prayer card before. Eventually we found out where the prayer card came from and how it materialized the day of my surgery.

Michael and Tara recently had moved into a new home. While packing, Michael noticed the prayer card at their old home. He was about to throw it away, but instead decided to "toss it" into a box of old toys that were to be packed for moving. This was back in January 2017. The toy box was then placed on an upper shelf of Lorenzo's bedroom closet in the new home. The particular toy box containing the prayer card had toys he hadn't played with in years! Yet that particular morning, our grandson asked for that particular toy box from the upper shelf! Thank God again! When the toy box was retrieved, he dumped it out on the living room floor, and out came the prayer card that had never been discarded. Lorenzo and his mom agreed that Beth should bring it to me in the hospital. It was another "gift" from God. We should all be as innocent as a child. This reminds me of what Christ said:

> *"Truly, I say to you, unless you turn and become like children, you will never enter the kingdom of heaven." (Matthew 18:3)*

So why are we to become children again? I think it is because we are all children of God. Children possess great qualities we somehow lose as we become adults. Children are trusting, innocent, humble, content with little pleasures, and most of all, they are awestruck! Christ further reminds us:

> *But Jesus said, "Let the children come to me, and do not hinder them; for to such belongs the kingdom of heaven." (Matthew 19:14)*

Sitting there with my wife and that prayer card that was somehow sent to us an hour before my ICD surgery, which had somehow been delayed five hours—well, go figure! All I knew was what it meant to me. My four-year-old grandson cared about his grandpa's well-being from a child's innocent perspective. I knew God sent the prayer card to me through Lorenzo.

My wife and I prayed the St. Anthony of Miracles prayer on the card, specifically asking that Dr. Srivathsan be able to feed the device wires through the coronary sinus veins. I then went to the cath lab to be prepped for the procedure. I kept thinking that God wanted me to go through another surgery. I had the crucifix in my right hand again, and like a child, I too was submitting to my Father's will. I had peace as I thought of heaven and the feeling of being home a week earlier.

As I was being wheeled into the surgery prep area, I heard the Spirit say within me, "Not all will believe and come to accept Me; each person has a choice to make." As my portable bed was locked in the cath lab prep area, a male nurse began to place an IV in my left arm. As he was doing so, another Mayo employee named Dan came up to me and asked if he could pray with me along with three other employees. He shared that he had heard about my miraculous recovery, and he reminded me of how great the Lion of Judah really is. I was so thankful for such faith-based medical personnel. Prayer builds confidence as faith is kindled. These four employees prayed many beautiful prayers over me, along with my family. Once again I prayed Romans 5:3–5, just as I had one week earlier.

When Dan and his prayer warriors began to pray, I noticed how uncomfortable the male nurse who was inserting the IV became. In fact, he got so uneasy that he left the area and only came back once they were finished praying. I felt very sorry for him not knowing how comforting and loving our Lord is. It was amazing how this occurred within minutes of the Holy Spirit reminding me that not all will believe in Jesus. We each have a choice to make.

After saying good-bye to my family, I was wheeled into the procedure room about 3:30 p.m. Dan continued to stay by my right side with comforting words. I held my crucifix in my right hand (again) and prayed. They told me that the procedure would start in about five minutes when Dr. Srivathsan arrived. I said okay and closed my eyes. Upon closing my eyes, I saw red again. It was an instant reminder to me that the Holy Spirit was indeed within me. I felt at total peace and knew that everything was in God's hands. Not only did faith and hope merge together, but trust in the Creator granted me peace.

I woke up to the anesthesiologist saying, "Wake up, Paul, and say something."

I immediately responded, "My crucifix."

He looked puzzled and said, "What did you say?"

I said again, "My crucifix."

A female nurse interjected, "I think he just said crucifix."

I nodded yes and added, "It was missing from my right hand."

They looked, and sure enough, it had fallen out of my hand. They gave it back to me. Yes, the first conscious thought I had upon awakening from the pacemaker and ICD implant procedure was the missing crucifix Beth had bought me. For some reason I felt a void only Christ could fill. While I was in recovery, Dr. Srivathsan told my family that he was able to thread the wire through the coronary sinus vein, but it was a dual tip lead (pacing and shock) and unfortunately when he tested the leads, only one worked. So he had to take it out, and he then used two leads for the ventricle through the veins and one for the atrium. He told my family, "I had to jerry-rig it to get it to work, but Paul is okay." Thank God for such a kind and good man. Thank God for gifted surgeons!

I was transferred to a regular bed on a different floor on Saturday. Very late Saturday night I was lying in bed alone. I recall trying to reason with God. I asked Him, "Why? Why did You allow this to happen to me? Why did my family have to personally witness this? Am I being punished for something I did or should have done?" These questions were all coming to the surface. All that happened was not supposed to occur as part of repairing the heart valve of a relatively healthy guy! I immediately caught myself and stopped questioning God. I realized to do so is sinful and from Satan.

> "For my thoughts are not your thoughts, neither are your ways my ways," says the Lord. For as the heavens are higher than the earth, so are my ways higher than your ways, and my thoughts than your thoughts." (Isaiah 55:8-9)

I apologized to God. He is the Potter, and I am the clay! I asked Him to remake me as a new pot to be used by Him. I reminded myself that God is a God of mercy and love. His will be done, not mine!

Alone in that dark hospital room, I became contemplative again and tried to listen again for His voice. In the silence, I recalled the two specific prayers I had prayed before the admission to Mayo. The first prayer was "Lord, I pray that whatever happens to me, may it strengthen my entire family's faith that they may know You are God. Also deepen their belief in the mercy, grace, and love of Jesus Christ and the power of the Holy Spirit. Most importantly, may they find salvation through faith and acceptance of Jesus as their personal savior." My second prayer was "Lord, Your will be done. But if I survive, I will evangelize and help bring souls to Christ while on earth."

The harvest is great, but the workers are few. Hope was now taking over. I felt His assurance that my prayers were truly answered. I sensed a renewed purpose for my human existence and life. Despite the whole ordeal, I felt blessed that I had grown spiritually.

On Sunday, June 11, 2017, I was discharged late in the afternoon. The doctors were amazed that I had not taken any pain medications. God spared me from physical pain. He is a gracious and loving God! Here I had open heart surgery, CPR administered on a new sternotomy, and continual defibrillations, and I never felt physical pain nor took pain medication.

We left the hospital about 5:00 p.m. and decided to spend the night next door at the Marriott Residence Inn. As I was wheeled out of Mayo in a wheelchair, I took my first breath of fresh air in ten days. Boy, did it feel good! I looked to the sky and thanked God I was alive. The things we take for granted!

CHAPTER EIGHT

SEARCHING FOR MEANING— FAITH UNDERSTOOD

For if you confess with your lips that Jesus is Lord and believe in your heart that God raised him from the dead, you will be saved. For man believes with his heart and so is justified, and he confesses with his lips and so is saved. The scripture says "No one who believes in Him will be put to shame. For there is no distinction between Jew and Greek; the same Lord is Lord of all, and bestows his riches upon all who call upon Him. For every one who calls upon the name of the Lord will be saved.
ROMANS 10:9–13

We drove home to Tucson on Monday, June 12, 2017. At first it was uncomfortable moving around. Normalcy wasn't quite there yet. My left arm was immobilized at night, and I wasn't allowed to lift my left elbow above shoulder level for four weeks so the wires in the pacemaker/ICD could solidify. Also I wasn't supposed to lift more than eight pounds. Tough to remember for a type A personality!

Sleeping was problematic, since I could only sleep on my back or on my right side. Thankfully the surgeon removed that lipoma from my right thigh. I guess God knows what we will need well in advance of us even knowing. The blessing of the lipoma removal proved necessary after the second pacemaker/ICD procedure. I could at least get some rest at night. Thank you again, God.

For the most part, though, things were going well. I was walking up and down the hallway of the house, as it was a modest 110 degrees outside. The discharge cardiac rehabilitation folks reminded me to walk as much as I could tolerate, but not outside in extreme heat. So, walking up and down the hallway of our house, I tried to get to 10,000 steps (about five miles) a day. Progress came in one-mile-per-day increments. I was starting to recover physically; mentally, however, it was very different.

Being human, I wondered what would happen if I had another cardiac arrest while I was home alone with my wife. I tried not to fixate on these thoughts, but they existed. I was physically sore and taking several medications—primarily heart medications and diuretics to remove fluids post-surgery—but no pain medication.

Three days later, at around 7:30 a.m., I got out of bed to go to the bathroom. I was extremely light-headed. While I was standing in the commode area, I felt like I was about to pass out. I struggled to remain standing. I tried to call for Beth. I didn't have the energy to yell her name; I just kept saying, "Beth, Beth, Beth," but knew she couldn't hear me. I began to panic. I thought to myself, *You cannot collapse! Your left arm is in a sling, you are on blood-thinning medication, and you cannot injure yourself.*

Totally panicked, I prayed, "Dear God, get me to the sink area so I can grab something to hold on to." As soon as my right hand clutched the countertop, I collapsed. My upper body shifted backwards against the wall, and

I fell straight down on my butt, using the wall to break the fall.

As I lay on the tile floor, my fear became outright terror. I desperately tried to keep my eyes open so I would stay conscious. I was facing the bathtub, and above it was a large, arched window with silhouette blinds that were drawn. As I struggled to keep my eyes open and stay conscious, I began to beg God to help me. I thought, *I don't know what is happening to me but the last time I closed my eyes involuntarily, I had a cardiac arrest. Something very serious is happening physically to me, and I am alone. I must muster strength to keep my eyes from shutting.* I also thought, *Perhaps my dear wife will find me unconscious or dead on the bathroom floor of our home.*

I prayed, "Please God, I don't know what is happening to me, but please help me—please!" My eyes were half closed, and as I looked up at the window above the bathtub, the same tremendous white light that I had witnessed during my cardiac arrests appeared again. I was awestruck. The brilliant white light was the only visible thing I saw. There was no bathtub window, no wall, no blinds, no tub—there was just the brilliant white light again!

Then I heard the Holy Spirit's voice say, "It's all right; you're okay; I have you." I felt a sense of great peace, and I closed my eyes. When I reopened them, the light was gone. I began to cry. God really does exist, and earnest prayer is powerful.

I composed myself, rested a minute, and then screamed for Beth. She came into the bathroom area and saw me on the floor, unable to get up. After several minutes she was able to help me into a sitting position. I told her I witnessed the same radiant light again, and I heard the Spirit tell me I was all right. We both sat there weeping.

Trusting what I heard in my inner being, I asked Beth to call the Mayo Clinic in Phoenix rather than 911. We called Mayo immediately, and Maggie McClain (she is a Godsend) called us back promptly. After listening to what happened physically, she asked what my weight was. I told her I had dropped three to four pounds per day since being home. She said, "You are most likely dehydrated with low electrolytes. Stop taking the diuretic medicine and the potassium pills immediately. Drink juice and hydrate, and call me back if you don't feel better or get coherent quickly." Great diagnosis and treatment plan! That's all it was, dehydration with low electrolytes. The second time I witnessed that pure light, I knew I wasn't crazy or hallucinating. It was real.

During the next several days, the inner voice kept directing me. While I was convalescing, I woke up in the middle of the night. This time, the inner voice instructed me to share with my brother Luke 6:37–38, which is a beautiful Scripture. I called him the very next day. I believed that my faith was somehow being proven or demonstrated to me. I was born an analytic and always asked "why." I also thought I had to figure things out and be data driven. It took a life-altering event to make faith a reality. Having a literal voice speaking into one's mind is a transcendent experience. It is beyond mental acuity and intellectual understanding.

On Monday, June 19, 2017, my sister Donna and her

husband Eric stopped by for a visit before heading to San Diego for a vacation. We talked about God's grace and his saving power. Donna also gave me a copy of all the prayers she said when I was having my cardiac arrests—specifically the ones she prayed on Sunday while she was in the waiting room, not knowing what was going on for hours.

As I was visiting with Donna, I began thinking about how Beth was going drive me to Phoenix the following Sunday for several follow-up appointments at Mayo on Monday, June 26, 2017. I became distracted and worried about my wife having to drive in the excessive heat on a Sunday to Phoenix with little road services being open. I thought about the tires on the car. Once again, the voice of God said to me in my mind, "Ask Eric to check the rear tires of the car you will take to Phoenix—specifically the inner part of the rear tires." I thought this was weird and also so precise in detail.

I looked at Eric and said, "Eric, before you leave, would you open the garage door and look at the rear tires on my car? Specifically, can you check the inside area of the rear tires by looking from under the car?" Eric asked me why and I told him I wanted to make sure the tires were safe in preparation for our trip to Phoenix. Eric went into the garage to inspect the tires, and he came back with an amazed look on his face. He said, "You are not going to believe this. You have a nail one inch from the inside of the right rear tire."

He went on to say, "Had the car *not* been parked exactly where it was in the garage, I might have never seen the nail." This event was a confirming moment for my family members and me. Someone (whom I call God) is really a part of me and watching over me. How many minor miracles do we overlook or simply ignore in our lives? Life does truly have meaning. I began to think, *I am not crazy. God is alive within me through his Holy Spirit and the mercy of Jesus Christ.* To say it succinctly, I am loved by an omniscient and omnipotent God.

> *Beloved, let us love one another, for love is of God; and he who loves is born of God and knows God. He who does not love does not know God, for God is love. (1 John 4:7–8)*

Beth took the car in and had the tires replaced for our trip. The specificity of God's directive to check our tires was mystical in nature. On Thursday, June 22, 2017, I was taking a shower about 4:00 p.m. While showering, I heard the voice again. "If someone suggests that you had an out-of-body experience, gently correct them and say that your soul left your body and that you were blessed to get a glimpse of heaven." Again, the words within my mind were so specific. I was getting used to the pattern that whenever I heard the voice, something relative to what I heard happened.

About forty minutes later, I was on the phone with John Marques, a dear friend who had moved to North Carolina three years earlier. I shared with him what had occurred medically and spiritually with me during the past month. When I got to the part about leaving my body and the light drawing and enveloping me, he interjected, "Paul, you had an out-of-body experience."

I literally had a "blink" moment as I recalled what was said to me in the shower forty minutes earlier. I replied, "My soul left my body, and I was blessed with a glimpse of heaven." Once again, my finite understanding of God and faith was being substantiated.

My post-surgical follow-up appointments at Mayo went well. Clinically or scientifically, the medical practitioners do not know why I kept having cardiac arrests after the surgical procedure to repair my mitral valve. Many simply said that it was a miracle that I was alive. I think it was simply God's will that I should remain for a while longer in the body. There must be more for me to do for His purpose.

Prior to going up to Phoenix for the medical appointments, I felt compelled to try and visit Bishop Olmsted personally to thank him for his prayers. I called his office and spoke to his assistant, Carmen. I explained what had happened to me and how the bishop had prayed for me. To put some context to my request for a personal visit with him, I suggested she share with Bishop Olmsted that on Pentecost Sunday at St. Paul's Church, a young man asked him for prayers for his father. I added to the request by saying, "I was the person they prayed for, and I wish to humbly thank him."

She made an appointment for Beth, Michael, and me to visit Bishop Olmsted on June 27. During our visit, I thanked him for praying for me with Michael on Pentecost Sunday. All three of us utterly admired his persona and presence. He truly is a man of God. He shared with us that he witnessed the sincerity of suffering and pain evident in our son that day. He went on to share with us that he was moved by Michael's outreach of faith in a time of crisis and remembered that they prayed together for me.

"Again (amen) I say to you, if two of you agree on earth about anything for which they ask, it will be done for them by my Father in heaven. For where two or three are gathered in my name, there am I in the midst of them." (Matthew 18:19–20)

"And whatever you ask in prayer, you will receive, if you have faith." (Matthew 21:22)

The bishop shared that when he returned to his residence that Pentecost Sunday, he continued to pray for me, especially during Midday Prayer and Vespers. I had such reverence for this man. While I was lying in an ICU on life support with treatment options waning, the Shepherd of the Catholic flock in Phoenix was praying for a stranger in his community.

The fact a bishop I had never met was involved in petitioning God, Jesus, and the Holy Spirit on my behalf is a profound blessing to me. There are no coincidences in life; it's all part of the Master's plan. His ways are beyond human understanding. How Michael crossed Bishop Olmsted's path that day via a phone message from his brother is divine intervention. I can never repay Bishop Olmsted for his prayers. I can only attempt to reciprocate by praying for him and his ministry. To that end, I continue to do so.

After visiting the bishop, Beth and I went back to the Mayo Hospital. We had written thank-you notes for the nursing staff in the ICU that took care of me weeks earlier. As I approached the hospital, I found myself not wanting to go in. Physical life and death happen there. Real pain and suffering occur inside those walls, and sometimes there is nothing clinical professionals can do to avert the death of somebody's loved one. As Beth and I walked through the doors, I looked up and said a solitary prayer for all the patients, families, and workers.

We went to the ICU on the second floor. The staff acknowledged us and allowed us to proceed to the nursing area. Beth and I visited with two of my nurses who were on duty that day. It was very emotional. We left the cards for those who were not on duty.

As we were leaving the ICU, Beth stopped and said, "Paul, that doctor over there was the physician who was at the head of your bed during your cardiac arrests." I had to acknowledge and thank him. I walked up to him and glanced for his name on his scrubs. I held out my hand and said, "Dr. McGarvey, my name is Paul Zucarelli, and I want to thank you for helping me when I was in your care a few weeks back." Yep, the same Dr. McGarvey I mentioned in Chapter 4.

As we shook hands, he seemed startled and stepped back a bit. He said he was happy to see me . . . pause . . . pause . . . upright! He then asked me if he could ask me a few questions. He said he had been "freaking out" thinking about me ever since I was discharged.

He went on to say, "Do you know what you said to

me?" and I replied, "Oh, you mean asking you if you used 150 joules on me when you wanted me to talk?"

What he said next stunned me. He said, "No, before that." He asked if I had time to chat now about this. I think we were both trying to figure out what happened—and more importantly, why.

He proceeded to ask me some very direct questions. "What was the last thing you saw before you went into the light and left the room?"

I replied, "The very last thing I saw was someone performing CPR on my body."

He said, "Okay, because that only happened once." He added, "Good—that is when you talked to us." He asked if I ever saw the defibrillating paddles or felt them. I said no; I left the room after the CPR. I also shared with him I didn't hear anything, just witnessed them around me in blue and green scrubs.

Dr. McGarvey then shared with me that while a patient is coding, his role is to manage the coded patient by standing at the head of the bed. He said he had kept his hand under my chin to ensure that my mouth stayed closed while he had a temporary airway and bag in the other hand. He said, "There is no way you can open your mouth while I am doing this."

He then shared that during that specific code, my eyes popped open. I stared at him and began to talk to him in a lockjaw-type of fashion (as he had my mouth held by the bottom of my jaw). He was surprised by this, and he said I was asking him what was going on. I said, "Leave me alone. I am fine!" Shaking his head and smiling, he finished by saying that was when they got a heart rate, and he removed his grip on my jaw and asked me to say something. That's when I asked if he had used 150 joules to defibrillate me.

Dr. McGarvey asked me, "Why did you ask me that question given that you never saw or felt the paddles associated with the defibrillation?"

I replied, "Doctor, I have *no* clue why I responded to you with that question! Perhaps the Holy Spirit was asking if you have faith." I added, "I don't know why I just said this." He smiled, we shook hands again, and I thanked him.

As I came home from the post-surgical visit and our meeting with Bishop Olmsted, I really felt at peace. There was deep meaning to life. I reflected on the calling to seek a second opinion, the disconcertedness in my soul leading up to surgery, the surgical "anomalies" that led to my heart to cease functioning, the steadfast faith of family and the Church continuing to intervene, and the amazing "voice" that guided my thinking and actions before they materialized in the natural order of people or events. When the voice speaks to me, these thoughts become front and center in my mind. It is as if all thought is wiped clean in my mind, and the only thought is someone speaking directly and literally into my brain. Whether it is Jesus, God, or the Holy Spirit, I honestly do not know. They are one to me in my faith.

I believe that my trials, afflictions, and personal sufferings were part of God's will and plan for me and others. I truly believe and accept this as fact. He strengthened me by instructing me to read Scripture before the ordeal. He also prepared me for hardships I would face by informing me that suffering was about to occur based upon the messaging in the Scriptures. But He also gave me peace of mind by constantly reassuring me, "Yes, you will suffer, but I am with you, and everything is going to be okay."

Now that I have passed through this valley, it has become clear to me. This journey was preordained. It's part of my life story. Christ suffered death on the cross for you and for me. Suffering is part of our earthly existence. Whether physically, emotionally, or mentally, we all will suffer while we are in the body. It is normal. Yet Christ suffered immensely, even dying for the sins of mankind, including my sins. These comforting and constant thoughts were embedded in my heart and mind and kept my faith strong. I continued to reflect on the light I saw and the incomprehensible feelings I had as my being was enveloped by that beautiful light.

And so, following Maggie McClain's suggestion, I have written down what has occurred so that my testimony may be memorialized for my family and others. I pray that it strengthens your personal faith and growth in your devotion and love for God, the Creator of the universe and the Creator of each of us. I specifically pray that you accept Jesus Christ as your personal savior and know that He was sent by God to redeem all those who choose to believe that Jesus is the Son of God who died, was resurrected from the dead, and is seated at the right hand of God. He will come again to judge all. I pray that all my family members' names are written in the Book of Life at the end of their earthly lives.

I also pray that anyone who hears or reads my testimony will have their existing faith strengthened. The Holy Spirit is alive and active if you tune out the busyness of your mind that focuses on "worldly things" and simply meditate on Him. Activate your spirit. God through Christ and the Holy Spirit wishes to "direct" your thoughts, activities, and speech. Think twice before you speak or act in haste, especially when what you say may cause hurt, pain, or intolerance toward another human being.

Many are the plans in the mind of a man, but it is the purpose of the Lord that will be established. (Proverbs 19:21)

Remember you are made up of three parts. Your body, or physical tent, is one part. Your soul, where your mind, emotions, and free will reside, is the second part of you. The third and most important part is your spirit. This is where you interact with God and come to know His presence. This spiritual realm can only become alive in you after accepting Jesus. You will have peace on earth, knowing eternity awaits you. Many of us don't think about death as we are caught up in living our daily lives. There is life after death, and it is eternal.

I encourage you to align your soul with God's true will, thus activating your spirit. We are all created for His purpose. What is more valuable or important? Getting to eighty years of earthly existence with lots of stuff? Or spending eternity in heaven amidst unconditional love with no pain, suffering, afflictions, disappointments, hurt, or sorrow?

I am so thankful that Beth purchased the crucifix for my journey. It serves as a constant reminder of Christ's unconditional love for me. I continue to rely on the fact Christ died, was resurrected, and promised me eternal life. He also promised me the Holy Spirit. The fact that the miracles occurred on Pentecost Sunday was not only symbolic but prophetic proof of the power of His Spirit. That crucifix embodies all this and more. It was my comfort in the storm, and it remains a comfort to me today.

> But God shows his love for us, in that while we
> were yet sinners, Christ died for us. (Romans 5:8)

I reflect now on how uselessly active I was prior to my health issues. I was so "busy" all the time in my mind! Not only accomplishing my to-do list, but simultaneously planning my next to-do list! I was constantly thinking, planning, and fretting.

My medical ordeal has been a blessing. The medical community calls it an anomaly; they do not know why it all happened. The experience has allowed me to move from my mind to focus instead on my soul and spiritual life.

The soul is your true self. The soul is where unbiased observation and true listening occur. Contemplation and discernment become real when the Spirit of the

Lord disarms all worldly matters. Also, in one's soul no judgments occur regarding others' actions or behaviors. You also stop judging yourself.

I no longer ask, "Why I am here? Do I matter?" This is passive thinking from the mind! God says, "I created you for a purpose. I have filled you with the Holy Spirit so you can lead a righteous and blessed life. I have given my only begotten Son to be Emmanuel (God with us)." By accepting Christ as our redeemer, we live for God's glory, not our own. With this freedom, we can readily help others, improve the human condition, and focus on the eternity of our souls while we are in the body on earth. We can't see what is on the other side of the mountain, but we know there is something beyond the slope we can see. In the same way, through faith we can know what is beyond our mortal life and existence. Perhaps that is why within the Lord's Prayer Jesus says, "Thy will be done on earth as it is in heaven." We are to seek His will "*while on earth*"—while in our physical bodies.

Although I had faith before my heart procedure, I now understand how real that faith is. The Holy Spirit became real and alive within me during my trials and suffering. The peace and comfort the Holy Spirit provided me is beyond comprehension. I know there is a God and heaven, and I know I will live eternally with him when I leave this earth. I pray that you'll join me in that belief.

God created each of us, and he loves each of us unconditionally. My journey has given me the opportunity to learn and grow in my knowledge of God with a deeper commitment to Jesus Christ. I also know the power of the Holy Spirit. All because of my human suffering! I know this is hard for many to grasp. But I am witnessing to this as truth. God has blessed me with my experiences to share with you. I personally witnessed the presence of heaven and felt at home where I truly belong.

We were created to serve God. Our human bodies or "tents" are temporary. They will wear out. Faith has to be the foundation of our existence, or life really has no meaning beyond a few decades of "existing." Perhaps this is why this world has so many man-made problems, mostly caused by our selfishness and pride. We cause our own sins not God.

God has truly blessed me and my family with so much provision, protection, and prosperity. Now looking back, every trial or suffering has prepared me for a deeper relationship with the Trinity. In other words, my sufferings and trials are preparing me for something even better—eternity in heaven. Perhaps without this suffering I would simply take God's blessings for granted. But now I know how good, kind, loving, merciful, and powerful God actually is. Medicine can only go so far. It is God who is the only true healer for those who unequivocally believe. I witnessed this through my mother's healing from cancer. Now it is my turn. I feel so much more secure now. I continually reflect on that "sight" and "feeling" of unconditional love when I was surrounded and embraced within the light. God has graced me with this demonstration of His love for me.

I have to mention again the crucifix Beth purchased

for me prior to the surgery. Having the cross reminded me that I too must carry my cross and I can bear all things in the body through Christ. If eternity is the desired state of my soul, the cross is the path there. During the hospital stay, I literally held that crucifix continually in my right hand, even while I slept at night with the necklace chain wrapped around my wrist. The redemptive suffering of Christ was my strength. Holding the cross, I knew Jesus suffered beyond human comprehension, dying for my sins and granting forgiveness to all who repent. My own forgiveness during my suffering has transformed me to be more forgiving of others.

My soul knows that unwavering faith in Jesus and the prayers of the faithful saved my human life. I now have a renewed purpose—*His purpose.* I look for ways in every interaction to help others grow their faith in God and Jesus. I wish to lead many to Christ and God's kingdom while on earth. I believe this is what he wants us all to do.

> *"The harvest is plentiful but the laborers are few; pray therefore to the Lord of the harvest to send out laborers into his harvest." (Matthew 9:37–38)*

I now realize I was allowed to live because my work here on earth is not yet complete from God's perspective. When His work is done through me, I will die and, in the blink of an eye, be back in His eternal paradise. I smile just thinking about and writing this.

I have come to know that all I really needed during

my surgery was my Bible, my crucifix, my unwavering faith in Jesus and the prayers of many faithful people. I am reminded that each day is a gift from God on our journey through our earthly existence. There is one scripture verse I've memorized that perfectly captures why faith matters:

*Without having seen him you love him; though you do not now see him you believe in him and rejoice with unutterable and exalted joy. **As the outcome of your faith you obtain the salvation of your souls.** (1 Peter 1:8–9, emphasis added)*

CHAPTER NINE

REFLECTIONS AND LESSONS LEARNED—
FOR HIS KINGDOM AND GLORY

I have been crucified with Christ; it is no longer I who lives, but Christ
who lives in me; and the life I now live in the flesh I live by faith in the
Son of God who loved me and gave himself for me.
GALATIANS 2:20

So what have I learned from this blessed experience?
What indelible mark has been left upon me as a child
of God? How shall I live the remaining days of my
human life? What do I wish my descendants to know
about Christ's great mercy and work within me so they
can experience it for themselves? How can I share my
experiences with others in order to help them genuinely
grasp faith? I have been pondering these questions for
months. Upon deep spiritual and intellectual reflection,
I've learned five key lessons from my experience.

Lesson 1 – Life Is a Gift

Prior to my medical events, I took a lot of my life for
granted. I was caught up in the busyness of life, as it is so
easy to do in our Western culture. It's all about activities
and experiences in our capitalistic environment. Life is

about always being active, going somewhere—but where? Doing things to do things. For me, it was not being able to sit still long enough to practice contemplative thinking focused on who we really are and what we should be doing with our finite time on earth. I had programmed my mind to think that if I just kept accomplishing my "to dos," somehow I would be worthy or recognized by others, especially by my friends and family. In essence, my self-worth came from earthly achievements. Our culture seems to reward this behavior. Glamour, financial success, capitalism—but to what end? Our culture teaches us to consume rather than simply be and give of ourselves. My achievements now pale in comparison to my community service work. Although I have done many things to help others, my mental to-do list never ceased. I literally would be planning my next "to dos" while checking off the boxes of my current "to dos." My life was activity-based.

I now view life as a precious gift from God. I no longer ponder why I am here. This is passive thinking. Instead of overthinking, I really believe in my heart that God created me for a purpose. I hoped this was the case, but I never really knew if it were true. After my medical trials, a dear spiritual mentor of mine, Fr. Patrick Kennedy, shared with me this quote: "A person's soul is one's only true self." Poignant and true.

I no longer fear death. Although my mind and body will wear out in the physical sense, I now know that my soul will live on. This spiritual perspective has given me clarity about what is really important. I believe the wonderful light that I was blessed to have witnessed twice is the Holy

Spirit. If one accepts that the soul is the true self of an individual, as Fr. Kennedy shared with me, then the soul is where unbiased observation occurs. In addition, in the soul, no judgments take place concerning other people's actions, comments, perceived intentions, or behaviors. We stop judging or condemning ourselves and others altogether. We can forgive others because we understand that He forgave us. By forgiving ourselves, we are free to forgive. As an added benefit, the grip of pride and self-absorption begins to loosen.

God loves us, and he empowers us to love others regardless of what they say or do. In the spiritual realm, true listening or discernment becomes real. The Spirit disarms all worldly matters and allows us to contemplate life's true meaning. We were all created by God, but why did he create us? Our lives are literally a gift. We need to use our time, talents, and earthly wealth to honor Him our Creator. I urge you to use your life to serve humanity and give glory to God.

I would encourage you to read Psalm 139. It is a beautiful psalm that describes how God knows each and every one of us. Read it and know you are known and loved.

With a grateful heart, I thank God for each day as I arise. I go to bed at night in prayer on my knees. I am now more acutely aware of other people's feelings and needs. I also have a more meaningful and highly personal relationship with Jesus Christ and the Holy Spirit. My priorities have changed. I dedicate time to thank God, talk to Him throughout the day, and ask Him to use me for His greater good while I'm alive on earth.

I will give thanks to thee, O Lord my God, with my whole heart, and I will glorify thy name forever. (Psalm 86:12)

I have also learned to be more compassionate and forgiving.

Lesson 2 – Faith Grows in Relationships

I believe we all are meant to have a relationship with God and His son, Jesus Christ. This is, in my opinion, how we can live a blessed life full of true happiness. When we live for God, it frees us from being controlled by our possessions and the interests of the self—bigger TVs, fancier cars, nicer houses, more clothes. We are all trying to fill a void that exists in each of us. No matter how hard we try to fill this void, we cannot. This void can only be filled by God.

I often say to my children and grandchildren, "If you believe it, you will see it." This is the antithesis of if you see it, you will believe it. Even one of Jesus's own, the Apostle Thomas said to his fellow disciples in doubt:

"Unless I see in his hands the print of the nails, and place my finger in the mark of the nails, and place my hand in his side, I will not believe." Jesus appeared to Thomas and said, "Put your finger here, and see my hands; and put out your hand and place it in my side; do not be faithless, but believing." Jesus continued to say to Thomas, "Have you believed because you have seen me? Blessed are those who have not seen and yet believe." (John 20:25, 27, 29)

Faith is the courage to believe and profess Christ indeed was crucified, resurrected, and is the intercessor for the salvation of our souls. Yet why is it so hard to believe? Is it that two thousand years have passed since Jesus lived on earth? Are we numb to the fact God created the universe and mankind? Is this why we are so selfish and try to be so self-sufficient?

Can you imagine a world where all humanity acted and behaved like Christ while He lived on earth? Think about it. Imagine how beautiful and peaceful the world would be if everyone actually practiced the Ten Commandments. These literal commands are God's directions concerning the way we should live and treat one another. I encourage you to read them or refresh your understanding of them. You will come to know God at a deeper level and have a joy-filled life if you practice them. I think that is what heaven is meant to be. Unfortunately we must each get through this earthly existence. Do we really want a deep relationship with God while here on earth? We all have free will and the ability to choose.

Reflecting again on my experiences, my journey has given me the opportunity to learn firsthand God's grace and love. It surpasses what one could ever hope or even imagine. I think about all the faithful people who prayed for me. Many are people whom I will never meet. Now that's faith—the ability to speak to God and ask Him to intervene for another human being. Remarkably beautiful. I now find myself praying more often for other human beings rather than just for my own intentions.

Now faith is the assurance of things hoped for, the conviction of things not seen. And without faith it is impossible to please him, for whoever would draw near to God must believe he exists and that he rewards those who seek him." (Hebrews 11:1, 6)

I continue to meet people every day, and I openly speak about my life and what has transpired. These people range from fellow Christians yet include atheists, agnostics, folks with diseases, and many ordinary people of all walks and ages. We talk about life and about how precious, yet fleeting, our time on earth truly is. We share our experiences, our beliefs, and our hopes and dreams. We talk openly about God and the preparedness of our souls when we die. Through relationships with other human beings, we become alive to the truth that we are all broken in some fashion. Yet faith holds the promise we all know exists in our hearts. Jesus promised us everlasting life.

Jesus said, "And I give them eternal life, and they shall never perish, and no one shall snatch them out of my hand. My Father, who has given them to me, is greater than all, and no one is able to snatch them out of the Father's hand. I and the Father are one." (John 10:28–30)

Serve others in deep relationships. As we care for each other's souls, our own faith will grow. Relationships with others and being in relationship with God and Jesus are systemically dependent on one another. If you have relationships that are damaged or have been ignored, repair and restore them. Simply take the initiative and trust in the Lord. In the Old and New Testaments, it says we are to love the Lord our God with all our heart, soul, mind, and strength, and love our neighbor as ourselves. The relationship between ourselves and God and humanity at large are interchangeable.

Lesson 3 – Prayer Matters to God

Every trial I've experienced has resulted in a deeper relationship with the Trinity. I now have an unprecedented appreciation of the absolute power of the Holy Spirit. My suffering created this metanoia within me. God has blessed me with the ability to share my experiences with you. I can now testify to what I have witnessed. Prior to surgery, I prayed when I faced times of uncertainty, despair, and pain. I prayed when I needed something or wanted to be heard. Although my mother was a testament of the power of prayer, I thought she was special in some way. I now have learned for myself that prayer does matter.

I prayed harder than ever prior to the surgery. I prayed for God's wisdom to be imparted to me. I prayed for forgiveness of all my sins. I prayed that I would survive. I acknowledged Jesus Christ as my personal Savior. I asked others to pray for me as well. People at work prayed for me. My family prayed for me; strangers and friends alike prayed for me. All these prayers continued during my cardiac arrests. As Michael's faith led him to seek God at church, the Spirit of the Lord sent him to meet Bishop Olmsted, who also prayed for me. A beautiful culmination of prayer on Pentecost Sunday. All glory to you, God.

Prayer matters to God. He listens to us. He yearns for a relationship with us. He desires us to talk to Him about everything in our lives. We matter to Him. As a child approaches a parent for guidance and direction, so too are we to approach God's throne of love, mercy, and grace as a child of God.

Prayer demonstrates gratitude and thankfulness. Many of us do not know how to pray. My advice to you is this: talk to Jesus as if He is your best friend. Share your whole story with Him. Talk regularly with Him. With practice, your faith will grow. For me, medical intervention only went so far. Prayer and intercession had to take over. God, Jesus, and the Counselor are healers beyond human capabilities for those who unequivocally believe.

"For I will restore health to you, and your wounds I will heal," says the Lord. (Jeremiah 30:17)

I now find myself talking to God quite often. I see Him in the ordinary beauty of the earth, the sky, wildlife, and all of creation. I find security in prayer as well. I continually recall the "light" I witnessed twice and the feeling of unconditional love I sensed as the light enveloped and embraced my being. My prayer life is more of gratitude and thanks versus wants and perceived needs.

If you recall, I prayed two simple prayers leading up to my heart surgery: 1) that all my family members would come to know and accept Jesus Christ as their personal Savior and that their names may be written in the Book of Life at the end of their earthly lives; and 2) that anyone who hears or reads my testimony will either come to personally know and accept Christ or have their existing faith strengthened and activated to help build God's kingdom while on earth. I am already seeing these prayers being answered in my family and others. If I believe in Christ, I must evangelize in His name.

"Whatever you ask in my name, I will do it, that the Father may be glorified in the Son. If you ask anything in my name, I will do it." (John 14:13–14)

Pray continually and earnestly. God listens. Be patient with yourself. Remember that all things work together for His good. As my mother used to say: "God doesn't always pay on Fridays, but He always pays on time—His time." If my experience has strengthened my own faith, I must bear witness to and for others. Evangelizing and discipleship for me are effortless now.

*Rejoice always, **pray constantly**, give thanks in all circumstances; for this is the will of God in Christ Jesus for you. (1 Thessalonians 5:16–18, emphasis added)*

Lesson 4 – Focus on Your Soul (Because in the End, It's All That Really Matters)

No one wants to die. Yet every human being will physically perish. Our modern culture teaches us to stay in shape, eat right, and spends billions of dollars on discretionary medical treatments and procedures to maintain the illusion of youth. Even the elderly are measured relative to the economic value or the cost to society to care for them. This is in stark contrast to the dignity and honor we should show the elderly for a life well lived.

Despite advances in medicine, our bodies eventually will wear out. Unlike any other creature, our minds have the ability to reason; free will enables us to choose among various options during our life. Our minds are active even while we sleep. Like our bodies, our minds can deteriorate over time. Today we have an epidemic of Alzheimer's disease and cognitive dementia as we age.

The soul is the only part of a person that lives on into eternity. I am convinced of this based upon my own experience. The Holy Spirit is active and alive if we seek God's voice and listen for His will for us. In other words, you have within you a part that has perpetual existence beyond physical death. We can be present where peace, joy and love reign. Isn't forever better than six, seven, or eight decades of human toil and struggle? So where should our focus be?

For me, I became aware of my soul when I accepted Jesus Christ. I didn't understand the profound positive impact this would have on my life until I faced the possibility of an earlier-than-normal death. All the "dots" in my life are truly connecting now. Life has profound meaning and purpose.

> *"But for this purpose have I let you live, to show you my power, so that my name may be declared throughout all the earth." (Exodus 9:16)*

Every human being has a soul and free will. By seeking God's direction in our lives, He prepares us for eternity in His kingdom. Your soul is where your thoughts, emotions, and free will reside. This is where you come to know, feel, and understand God's presence within us.

I believe this spiritual realm can only be present and tacit in an individual who has accepted Jesus Christ. Only when you explicitly understand and believe that eternity truly awaits can you have true peace while living here on earth. Your purpose on earth is to do God's will on earth while you are being prepared to serve Him forever in heaven. Life may be a journey, but heaven should be your goal or destination.

> *"I write this to you who believe in the name of the Son of God, that you may know that you have eternal life. And this is the confidence which we have in him, that if we ask anything according to his will he hears us." (1 John 5:13–14)*

> *"For God so loved the world that he gave his only Son, that whoever believes in him should not perish but have eternal life." (John 3:16)*

Doubt still plagues me at times. However, when doubt, uncertainty, or fear tries to invade my thinking, I go to my soul and reflect on the presence of the light and the radiating love I felt outside my body. We all have souls. Let us nourish them with prayer and gratitude to our Creator.

Lesson 5—There Is Salvation in Suffering

No one chooses to suffer, yet we all will suffer. This particular lesson is the most important one. If we diligently try to pattern our life after Jesus, we should strive to be as saint-like as possible. Why? Because a sanctified life lies between redemption and our entrance into God's heavenly kingdom.

The crucifix is a constant reminder of Christ's suffering for mankind. Christ knew what He was about to face—a brutally painful scourging and an agonizing death on the cross. He submitted to God's will, not His own. He freely offered His life for us. He bore our sins on that cross. We are redeemed.

With this in mind, I acknowledge all my physical frailties and afflictions. Yet I now refuse to allow them and any suffering that they may cause to deter me from the ultimate goal: the salvation of my soul. For me, the value of suffering is in the sanctification process while living. In layman's terms: no pain, no gain.

I must therefore embrace my cross daily; this is a symbolic metaphor to be Christlike while I live in my body. I must stay on the path to sanctity. For I know there is a paradise awaiting me. As Apostle Paul, in his final days, shared with a younger Timothy:

For I am already on the point of being sacrificed; the time of my departure has come. I have fought the good fight, I have finished the race, I have kept the faith. Henceforth there is laid up for me the crown of righteousness, which the Lord, the righteous Judge, will award to me on that day, and not only to me but also to all who have loved his appearing. (2 Timothy 4:6–8)

Suffering leads to salvation if we accept that suffering is a temporary and physical human condition. It is remedied by the promise of resurrection and eternal life. Despite my suffering, God chose to add days to my life. Perhaps it is because He wants me to evangelize to many and bring souls to Christ. Perhaps it is because He wanted me to write this book. Perhaps it is because He wants me to spread the good news and also alleviate some poverty or hunger before I go. Perhaps it is to teach the future generations about His omniscient glory and omnipresent love. Perhaps He simply wants me to try to live like Christ taught us to live.

There are questions I will never understand in this life. My mind cannot comprehend the mysteries of God. Yet I know my spirit witnessed something remarkable. My spirit was in the presence of a beautiful yet indescribable light. I am reminded often of this Scripture reference:

I shall not die but I shall live, and recount the deeds of the Lord. The Lord chastened me sorely but he has not given me over to death. (Psalm 118:17–18)

Any and all suffering is merely an opportunity to be more Christlike and stay focused on our salvation. Human or bodily suffering should only serve to remind us that our spiritual souls are soon to join the Lord. I cannot wait to be in the Light of God's presence again.

And I heard a voice from heaven saying, "Write this: "Blessed are the dead who die in the Lord henceforth." "Blessed indeed," says the Spirit, "that they may rest from their labors, for their deeds follow them!" (Revelation 14:13)

CHAPTER 10

LIVING NEW PATHWAYS

But the fruit of the Spirit is love, joy, peace, patience, kindness, goodness, faithfulness, gentleness, self control; against such there is no law. If we live by the Spirit, let us also walk by the Spirit.
GALATIANS 5:22–23, 25

Pentecost Sunday, 2018

It has been a year since the good Lord spared me through His love and grace. I initially struggled mentally to understand all that had happened. Why did this happen to me? What was I supposed to do with the rest of my life? But today I'm walking by the Spirit, discovering new pathways.

We had been trying to sell our home for three years as we wanted to downsize. We had taken our home off the market one week before my surgery. We listed it again after my surgery, and it sold in two weeks. God's timing is always the right timing! Beth and I decided to move from the Tucson area to the greater Phoenix area. In the Fountain Hills area we looked at five homes for rent and picked one. It took a half a day. We moved in late October 2017 after I had completed my cardiac rehabilitation.

The Sunday following our move, we went to the nearest church—St. Bernard of Clairvaux Catholic Church. *Clairvaux* means "the Valley of Light," and as we walked into the church for the first time, we were awestruck by the stained glass murals and scenes. To the right side of the altar, we gazed at an immense stained glass mural of Jesus raising Lazarus from the dead, one of Christ's greatest miracles.

This simple sight instantly made me weep. I felt God had literally picked our rental home so we would end up at this church. The scene is a constant reminder of His intervention in my healing. It was again confirmation from Him. I was where He wanted me to be.

Beth and I enjoyed the holidays with our children and grandchildren. I found myself being more passive than my previous self. I did more observing, listening, and reflecting on our family. I thought about how blessed I was to even be present this holiday season with the ones I love and cherish. I cannot stop thinking about heaven and how I felt. Nonetheless, I am still here.

We had found out that Bishop Olmsted was launching a campaign to evangelize and build discipleship in the Diocese of Phoenix. I wanted to honor my commitment that if I survived, I would evangelize for Christ and bring souls to Him. Beth and I got involved immediately. We have realized that God owns all our possessions. They are blessings from Him to be shared and used to help others in need. Despite being generous in the past, we have become more so now.

Meanwhile, I continued to write my story in hopes of

spreading the Gospel message well beyond my spheres of influence. In order to promulgate His love and glory, I also began to bear witness via in-person presentations to audiences of strangers. I spoke at churches, in people's homes, at restaurants over a meal, or wherever I was invited. It has been cathartic for me to tell my story in person and address specific questions and feedback from those who listen. The questions I receive are often about deepening one's faith.

Concerning my physical health, it took about six months to feel like I was somewhat physically normal. After six months, the physicians took me off all medications. I take a daily baby aspirin only. I do wonder how many more days the Lord will grant me to enjoy my family, raise awareness of His reality, and help bring many souls to Him before He calls me home (again). However, fully submitting myself to His will has granted me incredible peace of mind. I find myself speaking to the Trinity regularly. This occurs not only in prayer but also during times of normal daily mental thought or verbal conversations. When I speak to Him, I literally look up to the heavens. When I pray, I bow my head in thankful reverence to my Creator.

My prayers are very different these days. They used to be primarily about me and my needs. Now they are mostly about others and their needs. Perhaps it is because I know what I've witnessed; I know it's reality. The Lord has given this ordinary man who previously always needed to know "why" about everything an inner peace that can only come from Him. He handles the "whys"—not me.

I no longer need to understand everything. Every day I live is a day closer to my true home. I have resolved that He will take me home when His purpose for me on earth has been completed.

In January 2018 I had a follow-up visit with Dr. Srivathsan. He asked me if I knew how seriously ill I had been and if I remembered anything from June 4th (Pentecost Sunday). We spoke candidly as two close friends. He is a kind, humble, and wonderful human being as well as a skilled physician. He shared with me that the conventional treatment was not working and he knew he somehow had to get me to rest without my heart trying to beat on its own. He shared that he had done the ventricular ganglion nerve block on only one other patient in his career. He explained in layman's terms how he shut off my heart and lungs by anesthetizing the nerve. My heart and breathing then only occurred via machine while I rested. No one knew whether my heart would continue to go into cardiac arrest or be able to beat on its own in a regular fashion once the machines were turned off.

That evening after my visit with Dr. Srivathsan, I prayed. I asked God to help me understand from His perspective what had occurred and who was responsible for sparing my earthly life. The pieces were all there; I just needed to see the puzzle completed. Upon falling asleep that night, I had an incredible dream. In the dream, a man appeared to me whom I did not know. He wasn't clothed as an ordinary man, but was dressed in a white garment somewhat similar to a robe. He said to me, "Yes, my son, it was Dr. Srivathsan we sent to you in order to use his hands to spare your life while we heard the prayers being offered for you." This man kept repeating this to me over and over. Later, when I woke up, I immediately recalled the dream and shared it with Beth. I believe God was reconfirming that He used Dr. Srivathsan to save my life. I am now more motivated and energized to speak to people about the saving power of God since that dream.

As I live each new day, I try to live as much like Christ as I possibly can. After completely accepting God's will for me, I stay firmly planted on these new pathways by continually seeking His direction for my remaining days on earth. Many people have told me they have noticed a change in me. I strive to be more kind, humble, loving, and patient with everyone.

Looking back, I reflect on all the times I allowed events, circumstances, or people to irritate or bother me. In retrospect, the feelings I allowed to infiltrate my thoughts were meaningless and irrelevant when eternity became my focus and goal. Now I look for ways to help others with an emphasis on assisting people with their faith and spiritual development. As I immerse myself more deeply in God's Word, it provides literal nourishment for my body, mind, and soul. I often use Scripture to encourage people in need. Scripture has become a directional compass for me to live by. It is a road map that keeps me on the pathway of salvation.

I cannot wait to thank the good Lord again when I stand in His presence. I am grateful for His grace in my life. I love to spend time in prayer for my family as well as anyone else who is in need of prayer. While this has taken considerable discipline to incorporate into my daily routine, practice has made it reliable. I keep my heart and mind on Jesus Christ. The analogy I use to best describe this is: I keep one foot planted on earth and the other in transition to heaven. I call this "straddling" the physical world we live in with the true spiritual home we all long for.

> *But you beloved, build yourselves up on your most holy faith;*
> *pray in the Holy Spirit; keep yourselves in the love of God;*
> *wait for the mercy of our Lord Jesus Christ unto eternal life.*
> JUDE 1:20–21

EPILOGUE

Many say faith is a mystery. Yet I believe we all want to know that there is an eternal existence after this life. With new technologies and lifesaving methods, medical communities are bringing more and more people back from death. I am sure you have read other books or watched movies concerning the same topic.

I think every human being wishes to be loved. We all want to know that our life matters. We may be uniquely created as individuals, but we long for communion with one another. These are our intrinsic needs. The Apostle Paul figured this out a long time ago when he said he would show us a more excellent way to live—faith, hope, and love remain. But the greatest of these is love.

We were made for eternal life. This is our temporary home while in our body. There is a heavenly realm. Faith can be real in your life. I urge you to regularly pray and talk to God. Then simply listen and be aware of His voice in your life. He is waiting for you to trust Him and take the first step. You are known and loved by God. For Christians like myself, Jesus Christ is our personal Savior and God himself in human form.

When I die, I now have certainty that I will be welcomed in heaven and live on in spirit. I was an individual who always sought reason and knowledge to achieve understanding, but now I have been shown by God's grace what faith is all about. May the peace and grace and love of our Lord Jesus Christ be with your spirit. Faith is no longer a mystery to me for I have come to understand its meaning through my experiences. I pray my story will help you on your personal journey as we advance together to God's kingdom.

Peace and Grace to All!

ACKNOWLEDGMENTS

I am a truly blessed man. Regardless of how many more days of earthly existence the good Lord grants me, I know my soul will go on into eternity. I have been saved by the precious blood of Jesus Christ. I have the greatest possession on earth, a loving family.

To Beth, my one love. Thank you for the crucifix gift. Thank you for allowing Michael to leave my bedside on Pentecost Sunday to go to church. When he left in the midst of a crisis, you said, "He is in God's hands." You were prophetically correct!

To our son Michael. Thank you for following your calling to God and His Church. Your faith in action led you to Bishop Olmsted. You can always trust God.

To our son David. Your steadfast hand in tumultuous times demonstrates your love for family. Your phone message to Mike led him finally to St. Paul's and the bishop. Without you, my miracle may not have occurred.

To Steve, my only brother. I pray my journey has helped you carry your own cross. We will finish the race together, my beloved brother.

To Donna, my only sister. I knew there was a reason I asked you to be there for the surgery. Thank you for *all* the loving prayers! You are loved.

To Tara and Jonna: We are blessed to call you daughters. Thank you for loving Beth and me.

To Lorenzo: Thank you for the St. Anthony prayer card in your toy box and the bottle of Sprite! God has great plans for you.

To Suzan Martin: Thank you for all the typing, drafting, and love and support to make this book possible.

To Maggie McClain: Thank you for encouraging me to write my story. You planted the seed, and God watered it.

To Dr. Srivathsan: God used your skillful hands to spare my life on Pentecost Sunday. May God bless you my dear friend.

To the Mayo personnel: Thank you for *all* your care.

To our grandchildren: May this book be shared with you and our future generations so you too may know the love of God and your Savior Jesus Christ.

To everyone who prayed for me: God heard you! Thank You!

Know therefore that the Lord your God is God, the faithful God who keeps covenant and steadfast love with those who love him and keep his commandments, to a thousand generations.
DEUTERONOMY 7:9

written circa 1987/1988 PAZ

PAUL ZUCARELLI
PERSONAL MISSION STATEMENT

Please give a copy to my children & grandchildren so I share w them "who" I was and Am.

Paul

Born: <u>April 15, 1959</u>   Died: _____

- I will live my days free from hate, greed, and evil.

- I will be a companion and guardian to my wife, but most importantly, her best friend.

- I will be a brother to all men, but especially to my only God given brother and sister.

- I will teach my children charity, thankfulness, and the ability to hope and dream.

- As a father, I will strive to ensure that my children have instilled in them Christian values of morality, compassion and forgiveness. Above all, I will strive to teach them to love God with all their heart, mind, and soul, and accept Jesus as their savior so that they may have eternal life.

- I will continually ask God for strength to maximize the utilization of my talents and fulfill my responsibilities. In him rests my security.

- I will strive to leave something positive with every person I meet.

- I will live my life debt free beginning at age 40.

- I will provide guidance to my parents, as they guided me in my youth.

- In whatever field of endeavor I partake, I shall work to leave the situation better than when I arrived, while at no one's expense.

- I will take the time to relax and reflect in order that my spirit matures.

PAUL ZUCARELLI
PERSONAL MISSION STATEMENT

<u>Updated 3/4/2007</u>

- I will focus my energies on my Lord and Savior to improve my daily walks with him (John 3:30)

- I will provide adult mentoring to my adult children so the roads they travel in life may be smooth and I will help them find their purpose.

- I will provide for my mother, wife, brother, and sister regardless of their needs. I will do the same for my children and grandchildren.